"Be courageous about and focus on your goals the way runners and bikers focus on the finish line, the way swimmers focus on form and speed, the way mountain climbers focus on the top, and the way ball players focus on upping the score. Work on creating your goals into reality the way classical musicians organize musical notes to make beautiful sound: That is, through thoughts and actions called *practice*. Within the bravery of courage in action is the beauty of elegance in practice."

– John McCabe, from his book *Igniting Your Life*

# Books by John McCabe

**Igniting Your Life:**
Pathways to the Zenith of Health and Success

**Voices of Reason**
Quotations of Uplifting and Motivational
Philosophy from throughout History

**Voices of Wisdom**
Quotations of Uplifting and Motivational
Philosophy from throughout History

**Voices of Insight**
Quotations of Uplifting and Motivational
Philosophy from throughout History

**Arise**
Recovering, Revealing, and Ascending
into the Law of Manifestation

**Sunfood Diet Infusion:**
Transforming Health and Preventing
Disease through Raw Veganism

**Raw Vegan Easy Healthy Recipes:**
Simple, Low-fat, Health Infusing Cuisine

**Vegan Truth Vegan Myth:**
Obliterating Rumors and Lies about the Earth-Saving
Diet that can Save Your Life

**Extinction:**
The Death of Waterlife on Plan

"Never let the future disturb you. You will meet it, if you have to, with the same weapons of reason which today arm you against the present."
– Marcus Aurelius

# Voices of
# Reason

## Quotations of Uplifting & Motivational Philosophy from throughout History

## John McCabe

### Author of
### *Igniting Your Life*

# Voices of Reason

## Disclaimer:

**ISBN:** 978-1-884702-17-4
First Edition: 2015

## Copyright © 2014 by John McCabe

For Diane.

"Those who will not reason are bigots, those who cannot are fools, and those who dare not are slaves."
– George Gordon Byron

# INTRODUCTION

I began collecting quotations when I was a teenager. I had not idea that my collection would someday climb into the thousands.

At first, I was seeking life advice. Being one who came from a dramatically dysfunctional household of many troubles, I did not receive any life guidance. By the time I was out of high school, I felt I had been spit out into the world with nary a morsel of life advice to nibble from.

As I began working at sometimes three low-paying jobs at a time to get by, I knew that the life I was leading was no way to be living. I had a strong desire to improve my situation. I began reading books and digging through the daily newspapers and weekly and monthly publications trying to find my way, looking for what I thought I needed to know. As I read, I often made notes of what I found to be interesting, and many of those notes ended up as quotations in this book.

I had a girlfriend in college who knew of my file box of quotations, and she started collecting quotations and slipping them in my file. Other people also knew of my little hobby and sometimes gave or sent me quotations they thought interesting.

Rather than try to classify each quotation in this book, I simply alphabetized them by author. Someone said to me that it would have been more helpful if I had little information about each person being quoted. That would have made the book at least twice as thick, and a project that would have taken a very long time to compile. I thought the book should simply be about the quotations, the theories and concepts they propose, and, most of all, the thoughts those quotations stir in the reader. I don't think that, for the reader, the issue should be about what the person being quoted was thinking. Instead, I thought the book should be more about and for the actual reader, and how the quotations trigger their thoughts.

I hope you can find inspiration, motivation, enlightenment, and even humor in the quotations I have compiled.

# A

"Somewhere in the depths of solitude, beyond wilderness and freedom, lay the trap of madness."
– Edward Abbey

"What we need now are heroes and heroines, about a million of them. One brave deed is worth a thousand books. Sentiment without action is the ruin of the soul."
– Edward Abbey

"You live in a pulsating, vibrating Universe of advanced harmonics. Everything that exists, in your air, in your dirt, in your water, and in your bodies, is vibration in motion—and all of it is managed by the powerful Law of Attraction. There is nothing that exists outside of this vibrational nature, and as you learn to accept your vibrational nature, and begin to consciously utilize your emotional vibrational indicators, you will gain conscious control of your personal creations and of the outcomes of your life experience."

– Abraham-Hicks

"You are meant to succeed, and failure should feel bad to you. Life is supposed to go well for you - and when it does not, there is something wrong. But what is wrong is not something that is outside of you over which you have no control. What is wrong is within you - and you do have control."

– Abraham-Hicks

"The biggest challenge for most spiritual seekers is to surrender their self importance, and see the emptiness of their own personal story. It is your personal story that you need to awaken from in order to be free."

– Adyashanti

"Life is your art. An open, aware heart is your camera. A oneness with your world is your film."

– Ansel Adams

"There is no such thing as a 'self-made' man. We are made up of thousands of others. Everyone who has ever done a kind deed for us, or spoken one word of encouragement to us, has entered into the make-up of our character and of our thoughts, as well as our success."

– George Burton Adams

"Encouragement is the oxygen of the soul."
– George M. Adams

"To achieve greatness, you must be prepared to dabble on the boundary of disaster."
– Henry Adams

"If your actions inspire others to dream more, learn more, do more, and become more, you are a leader."
– John Quincy Adams

"Remember there's no such thing as a small act of kindness. Every act creates a ripple with no logical end."
– Scott Adams

"The good we secure for ourselves is precarious and uncertain until it is secured for all of us and incorporated into our common life."
– Jane Addams

"Our greatest blessings often appear to us in the shape of pains, losses, and disappointments; but let us have patience and we soon shall see them in their proper figures."
– Joseph Addison

"The hero is the one who kindles a great light in the world, who sets up blazing torches in the dark streets of life for men to see by. The saint is the man who walks through the dark paths of the world, himself a light."
– Felix Adler

"Make no mistake about it – enlightenment is a destructive process. It has nothing to do with becoming better or being happier. Enlightenment is the crumbling away of untruth. It's seeing through the façade of pretense. It's the complete eradication of everything we imagined to be true."
– Adyashanti

"Gratitude is the sign of noble souls."
– Aesop

"Sometimes, people can go missing right before our very eyes. Sometimes, we los sight of ourselves when we're not paying enough attention."
– Cecelia Ahern

"Painful as it may be, a significant emotional event can be the catalyst for choosing a direction that serves us - and those around us - more effectively. Look for the learning."
– Louisa May Alcott

"In selling as in medicine, prescription before diagnosis is malpractice."
– Tony Alesandra

"I do not choose to be a common man. It is my right to be uncommon – if I can. I seek opportunity – not security. I do not wish to be a kept citizen, humbled and dulled by having the state look after me. I want to take the calculated risk; to dream and to build, to fail and to succeed. I refuse to barter incentive for a dole. I prefer the challenges of life to the guaranteed existence; the thrill of fulfillment to the stale calm of utopia. I will not trade freedom for beneficence nor my dignity for handout. I will never cower before any master nor bend to any threat. It is my heritage to stand erect, proud and unafraid; to think and act for myself, enjoy the benefit of my creations, and to face the world boldly and say, this I have done."
– Dean Alfange

"Champions aren't made in gyms. Champions are made from something they have deep inside them – a

desire, a dream, a vision. They have to have the skill, and the will. But the will must be stronger than the skill."
– Muhammad Ali

"I know where I'm going and I know the truth, and I don't have to be what you want me to be. I'm free to be what I want. And I know service to others is the rent you pay for your room here on Earth."
– Muhammad Ali

"Great flame follows a tiny spark."
– Dante Alighieri

"People of mediocre ability sometimes achieve outstanding success because they don't know when to quit. Most men succeed because they are determined to."
– George Allen

"Jumping at several small opportunities may get us there more quickly than waiting for one big one to come along."
– Hugh Allen

"You cannot escape the results of your thoughts. Whatever your present environment may be, you will fall, remain, or rise with your thoughts, your vision, your ideal. You will become as small as your controlling desire; as great as your dominant aspiration."
– James Allen

"You will become as small as your controlling desire; as great as your dominant aspiration."
– James Lane Allen

"The only competition worthy of a wise man is with himself."
– Washington Allston

"For away there in the sunshine are my highest aspirations. I may not reach them, but I can look up and see their beauty, believe in them, and try to follow where they lead."
– Louisa May Alcott

"We all have our own life to pursue, our own kind of dream to be weaving, and we all have the power to make wishes come true, as long as we keep believing."
– Louisa May Alcott

"There is not enough darkness in all the world to put out the light of even one small candle."
– Robert Alden

"Do not count the days; make the days count."
– Muhammad Ali

"One of the most difficult things everyone has to learn is that for your entire life you must keep fighting and adjusting if you hope to survive. No matter who you are or what your position is you must keep fighting for whatever it is you desire to achieve."
– George Allen

"Doing easily what others find difficult is talent; doing what is impossible for talent is genius."
– Henri-Frederic Amiel

"Life is short and we have never too much time for gladdening the hearts of those who are traveling the dark journey with us. Oh be swift to love, make haste to be kind."
– Henri-Frederic Amiel

"Learn to limit yourself; to content with yourself with some definite work; dare to be what you are and learn to resign with a good grace all that you are not; and to believe in your own individuality."
– Henri-Frederic Amiel

"The man who insists upon seeing with perfect clearness before he decides, never decides."
– Henri Frederic Amiel

"Don't ever let an airplane take you someplace where your brain hasn't arrived at least a couple of minutes earlier."
– Andy Anderson

"Only one thing has to change for us to know happiness in our lives: where we focus our attention."
– Greg Anderson

"When people don't express themselves, they die one piece at a time."
– Laurie Halse Anderson

"Our lives improve only when we take chances – and the first and most difficult risk we can take is to be honest with ourselves."
– Walter Anderson

"Perseverance is failing 19 times and succeeding the 20th."
– Julie Andrews

"Each of us has that right, that possibility, to invent ourselves daily. If a person does not invent herself, she will be invented. So, to be bodacious enough to invent ourselves is wise."
– Maya Angelou

"The best part of life is not just surviving, but thriving with passion and compassion and humor and style and generosity, and kindness."
– Maya Angelou

"Love recognizes no barriers. It jumps hurdles, leaps fences, penetrates walls to arrive at its destination, full of hope."
– Maya Angelou

"A bird doesn't sing because it has an answer, it sings because it has a song."
– Maya Angelou

"Do the best you can until you know better. Then when you know better, do better."
– Maya Angelou

"It is time for parents to teach young people early on that in diversity there is beauty and there is strength."
– Maya Angelou

"It is time for parents to teach young people early on that in diversity there is beauty and there is strength."
– Maya Angelou

"The ache for home lives in all of us, the safe place where we can go as we are and not be questioned."
– Maya Angelou

"My mission in life is not merely to survive, but to thrive; and to do so with some passion, some compassion, some humor, and some style."
– Maya Angelou

"Without courage, we cannot practice any other virtue with consistency. We can't be kind, true, merciful, generous, or honest."
– Maya Angelou

"Confrontation should always leave a person's dignity in tact."
– Dr. A.J. Anglin

"The things I learned from my experience in music in school are discipline, perseverance, dependability, composure, courage, and pride in results. Not a bad preparation for the workforce!"
– Gregory Anrig

"I have never been a millionaire. But I have enjoyed a great meal, a crackling fire, a glorious sunset, a walk with a friend, a hug from a child, a cup of soup, a kiss behind the ear. There are plenty of life's tiny delights for all of us."
– Jack Anthony

"If you don't change your beliefs, your life will be like this forever. Is that good news?"
– Dr. Robert Anthony

"Consider how much more you often suffer from your anger and grief, then from those very things for which you are angry and grieved."
– Marcus Antonius

"Now and then it's good to pause in our pursuit of happiness and just be happy."
– Guillaume Apollinaire

"I have heard it said that the first ingredient of success – the earliest spark in the dreaming youth is this: dream a great dream."

– John A. Appleman

"Make choices that are loving for yourself with your diet, your relationships, and in speaking your loving truth."

– India.Arie

"It is the mark of an educated mind to be able to entertain a thought without accepting it."

– Aristotle

"We can experience any kind of pleasure and pain either too much or too little. But to experience all this at the right time, toward the right objects, toward the right people, for the right reason, and in the right manner – that is the median and the best course, the course that is a mark of virtue."

– Aristotle

"I believe every human has a finite number of heartbeats. I don't intend to waste any of mine."

– Neil Armstrong

"Giving is a universal opportunity. Regardless of your age, profession, religion, income bracket, and background, you have the capacity to create change."

– Laura Arrillaga-Andreesen

"Shun idleness. It is a rust that attaches itself to the most brilliant of metals."

– François-Marie "Voltaire" Arouet

"What you are in love with, what seizes your imagination, will affect everything. It will decide what

gets you out of bed in the mornings, what you do with your evenings, how you spend your weekends, what you read, who you know, what breaks your heart, and what amazes you. Fall in love, stay in love, and it will decide everything."
– Pedro Arrupe

"Aerodynamically the bumblebee shouldn't be able to fly, but the bumblebee doesn't know that so it goes on flying anyway."
– Mary Kay Ash

"From what we get, we can make a living; what we give, however, makes a life."
– Arthur Ashe

"Start where you are. Use what you have. Do what you can."
– Arthur Ashe

"One reason I don't drink is that I want to know when I am having a good time."
– Lady Astor

"Thousands have lived without love, not one without water."
– W.H. Auden

"Since nothing we intend is ever faultless, and nothing we attempt ever without error, and nothing we achieve without some measure of finitude and fallibility we call humanness, we are saved by forgiveness."
– David Augsburger

"Faith is to believe what you do not yet see; the reward for this faith is to see what you believe."
– Saint Augustine

"Do you wish to be great? Then begin by being. Do you desire to construct a vast and lofty fabric? Think first about the foundations of humility. The higher your structure is to be, the deeper must be its foundation."

– Saint Augustine

"Will is to grace as the horse is to the rider."

– Saint Augustine

"Love and do what you will."

– Saint Augustine

"Waste no more time arguing what a good man should be. Be one."

– Marcus Aurelius

"He who lives in harmony with himself lives in harmony with the universe."

– Marcus Aurelius

"When force of circumstance upsets your equanimity, lose no time in recovering your self-control and do not remain out of tune longer than you can help."

– Marcus Aurelius

"Approval itself doesn't improve something. To expect a special reward for doing your work is like your eye demanding a reward because it sees, or your feet because they walk."

– Marcus Aurelius

"Our anger at others often wounds us worse than the things about which we are angry. Where is the anger for your own lack of foresight in avoiding the injury?"

– Marcus Aurelius

"Work at what's in front of you with the tools you have, shrinking from nothing, following right reason and moving towards a more integrated life. Do it vigorously and with no distractions, yet calmly and with all of your love and humor."

– Marcus Aurelius

"There is nothing I would not do for those who are really my friends. I have no notion of loving people by halves, it is not in my nature."

– Jane Austen

"Friendship, love, health, energy, enthusiasm, and joy are the things that make life worth living and exploring."

– Denise Austin

"You are here for a purpose. There is no duplicate of you in the whole wide world. There never has been, there never will be. You were brought here now to fill a certain need. Take time to think that over."

– Lou Austin

"The bird dares to break the shell, then the shell breaks open and the bird can fly openly. This is the simplest principle of success. You dream, you dare, and you fly."

– Israelmore Ayivor

"I do believe that when we face challenges in life that are far beyond our own power, it's an opportunity to build on our faith, inner strength, and courage. I've learned that how we face challenges plays a big role in the outcome of them."

– Sasha Azevedo

# B

"Simplicity boils down to two steps: Identify the essential. Eliminate the rest."
– Leo Babauta

"The bond that links your true family is not one of blood, but of respect and joy in each other's life. Rarely do members of one family grow up under the same roof."
– Richard Bach

"Who questions much, shall learn much, and retain much."
– Francis Bacon

"It is true, that a little philosophy inclineth man's mind to atheism, but depth in philosophy bringeth men's minds about to religion."
– Francis Bacon

"As the crisis of feeding the World's population grows, breeding of animals for human consumption becomes less acceptable — out of compassion for the suffering of animals and the awareness that it is a grossly inefficient use of water and grain. A new relationship with the animal kingdom is part of our changing perception of the Earth. Animals are part of us, and part of our practice."
– Allan Hunt Badiner

"Actions is the antidote of despair."
– Joan Baez

"Don't adventures ever have an end? I suppose not. Someone else always has to carry on the story."
– Bilbo Baggins

"Flying is so many parts skill, so many parts planning, so many parts maintenance and so many parts luck. The trick is to reduce the luck by increasing the others."
– David L. Baker

"Vision without action is merely a dream. Action without vision just passes the time. Vision with action can change the world."
– Joel A. Baker

"Surely the day will come when color means nothing more than skin tone, when religion is seen uniquely as a way to speak one's soul; when birth places have the

weight of a throw of the dice, and all men are born free, when understanding breeds love and brotherhood."
– Josephine Baker

"Most people are like you and me, or the people across the street or around the world from you and me. Just like you and me, their hearts tell them that somewhere, somehow, they can make a positive difference in the world."
– William Baker

"Not everything that is faced can be changed. But nothing can be changed until it is faced."
– James Baldwin

"Nothing is more desirable than to be released from an affliction, but nothing is more frightening than to be divested of a crutch."
– James Baldwin

"I don't know anything about luck. I've never banked on it, and I'm afraid of people who do. Luck to me is something else; hard work and realizing what is opportunity and what isn't."
– Lucille Ball

"I have an everyday religion that works for me. Love yourself first, and everything else falls into line. You really have to love yourself to get anything done in this world."
– Lucille Ball

"A human body and a bicycle are the perfect synthesis of body and machine."
– Richard Ballantine

"The cruelties associated with the slaughter of the animal kingdom for human consumption, the pain, fear, and distress suffered by the animals in the entire process of being fattened for butchering, as well as the environmental disasters wreaked upon our planet through the meat industry, are very well documented, and should be understood by all who claim to be developing the enlightenment, or who wish to."
– Bodo Balsys

"My responsibility to myself, my neighbors, my family and the human family is to try to tell the truth."
– Toni Cade Bambara

"If you wait until you can do everything for everybody, instead of something for somebody, you'll end up not doing nothing for nobody."
– Malcom Bane

"Nobody can be exactly like me. Sometimes even I have trouble doing it."
– Tallulah Bankhead

"You just have to trust your own madness."
– Clive Barker

"Vision without action is merely a dream. Action without vision just passes the time. Vision with action can change the world."
– Joel A. Barker

"I don't know anybody's road who's been paved perfectly for them, there are no manuals, you don't know what life has in store for you."
– Drew Barrymore

"Opinions that are well rooted should grow and change like a healthy tree."
– Irving Batcheller

"Praise can be your most valuable asset, as long as you don't aim it at yourself."
– Orlando A. Battista

"Inspiration comes of working every day."
– Charles Baudelaire

"Let us have a care to disclose our hearts to those who shut up theirs against us."
– Francis Beaumont

"Be daring, be different, be anything that will assert integrity of purpose and imaginative vision against the play-it-safers."
– Cecil Beaton

"Live your life from your heart. Share from your heart. And your story will touch and heal people's souls."
– Melody Beattie

"Gratitude unlocks the fullness of life. It turns what we have into enough, and more. It turns denial into acceptance, chaos to order, confusion to clarity. It can turn a meal into a feast, a house into a home, a stranger into a friend."
– Melody Beattie

"Strength is a matter of the made-up mind."
– John Becker

"Impossible is just a big word thrown around by small men who find it easier to live in the world they've been given than to explore the power they have to

change it."
— David Beckham

"You bring out the best in yourself by looking for the best in others."
— Gene Bedley

"There are only two lasting bequests we can hope to give our children. One of these is roots, the other, wings."
— Henry Ward Beecher

"Hold yourself to a higher standard than anyone else expects of you. Never excuse yourself."
— Henry Ward Beecher

"It's easier to go down a hill than up it, but the view is much better at the top."
— Henry Ward Beecher

"Courage is the ladder on which all the other virtues mount."
— Brandon Francis Behan

"Concentrate all your thoughts upon the work at hand. The sun's rays do not burn until brought to a focus."
— Alexander Graham Bell

"When one door closes, another opens; but we often look so long and so regretfully upon the closed door that we do not see the one which has opened for us."
— Alexander Graham Bell

"The most sacred place in the world is your mind. Guard it ferociously."
— Rick Beneteau

"As a minister, I experienced the power of industrialists and bankers to get their way by use of the crudest form of economic pressure, even blackmail, against a Labour Government. Compared to this, the pressure brought to bear in industrial disputes is minuscule. This power was revealed even more clearly in 1976 when the IMF secured cuts in our public expenditure. These lessons led me to the conclusion that the UK is only superficially governed by MPs and the voters who elect them. Parliamentary democracy is, in truth, little more than a means of securing a periodical change in the management team, which is then allowed to preside over a system that remains in essence intact. If the British people were ever to ask themselves what power they truly enjoyed under our political system they would be amazed to discover how little it is, and some new Chartist agitation might be born and might quickly gather momentum."

– Tony Benn

"It's easier to go down a hill than up it but the view is much better at the top."

– Arnold Bennet

"The secret of getting ahead is getting started."

– Sally Berger

"If opportunity doesn't knock, build a door."

– Milton Berle

"In every situation, no matter how horrifying it may be, we have a choice: the choice to see love instead of fear."

– Gabrielle Bernstein

"Baseball is ninety percent mental. The other half is physical."
– Yogi Berra

"I didn't say the things I said."
– Yogi Berra

"If you don't know where you are going, you might wind up someplace else."
– Yogi Berra

"We've been caught up in a mechanical world, because what we make, makes us. We make the automobile, the automobile makes us. We make an industrial economy, the industrial economy makes us. We are now in a weird dream world of industrial technological imagination. Who would be so destructive to the very bases out of which we exist, that we spoil our water and our air? For what? To invent an industrial economy. We are so brilliant scientifically and so absurd in any other way. We are into a deep cultural pathology – in ordinary language, we are crazy. To think that we can have a viable human economy by destroying the Earth economy is absurd."
– Thomas Berry

"It may be that when we no longer know what do to, we have come to our real work, and when we no longer know which way to go, we have begun our real journey."
– Wendell Berry

"It is not from ourselves that we learn to be better than we are."
– Wendell Berry

"Invest in the human soul. Who knows, it might be a diamond in the rough."
– Mary McLeod Bethune

"Whatever I am offered in devotion with a pure heart – a leaf, a flower, fruit, or water – I accept with joy."
– Bhagavad Gita

"What is work and what is not work are questions that perplex the wisest of men."
– Bhagavad Gita

"Human life is meant for a little austerity. We have to purify our existence; that is the mission of human life … because then you will get spiritual realization, the unlimited, endless pleasure and happiness. That is real pleasure, real happiness."
– A.C. Bhaktivedanta

"Blessed are those who can give without remembering and take without forgetting."
– Elizabeth Bibesco

"Consider the postage stamp: it's usefulness consists in the ability to stick to one thing till it gets there."
– Josh Billings

"I don't care how much a person talks, if they only say it in a few words."
– Josh Billings

"Occasions are rare; and those who know how to seize upon them are rarer."
– Josh Billings

"Spirituality is about joy, fun, creating, and playing. It is absolutely not rigid, full of rules, or judgmental. It is about freedom, love, and laughter."

– Karen Bishop

"Great changes may not happen right away, but with effort even the difficult may become easy."

– Bill Blackman

"Mutual forgiveness of each vice, such are the gates of paradise."

– William Blake

"We should cultivate the ability to say no to activities for which we have no time, no talent, and which we have no interest or real concern. If we learn to say no to many things, then we will be able to say yes to the things that matter most."

– Roy Blauss

"Once you stop clinging and let things be, you'll be free. You'll transform everything. And you'll be at peace wherever you are."

– Bodhidharma

"Your greatness is measured by your kindness; your education and intellect by your modesty; your ignorance is betrayed by your suspicions and prejudices, and your real caliber is measured by the consideration and tolerance you have for others."

– William J.H. Boetcker

"That you may retain your self-respect, it is better to displease the people by doing what you know is right, than to temporarily please them by doing what you know is wrong."

– William J.H. Boetcker

"We think sometimes that poverty is only being hungry, naked, and homeless. The poverty of being unwanted, unloved, and uncared for is the greatest poverty. We must start in our own homes to remedy this kind of poverty."
– Anjeze Gonzhe "Mother Teresa" Bojaxhiu

"A man must drive his energy, not be driven by it."
– William Frederick Book

"In life, it is never the big battle, the big moment, the big speech, the big election. That does not change things. What changes things is every day, getting up and rendering small acts of service and love beyond that what's expected of you or required of you."
– Cory Booker

"Laughter is the shortest distance between two people."
– Victor Borge

"The difference between greatness and mediocrity is often how an individual views a mistake."
– Nelson Boswell

"There are two ways of meeting difficulties. You alter the difficulties or you alter yourself to meet them."
– Phyllis Bottome

"If you concentrate on yourself, you can change the world."
– Victoria Boutenko

"When there is no where else to turn, turn inward. Enter into the sacred silence of your soul and ask for healing, guidance, and personal peace."
– Michaiel Bovenes

"Flying is hours and hours of boredom sprinkled with a few seconds of sheer terror."
– Gregory "Pappy" Boyington

"What makes a river so restful to people is that it doesn't have any doubt. It is sure to get where it is going, and it doesn't want to go anywhere else."
– Hal Boyle

"I know you've heard it a thousand times before. But it's true – hard work pays off. If you want to be good, you have to practice, practice, practice. If you don't love something, then don't do it."
– Ray Bradbury

"There are worse crimes than burning books. One of them is not reading them."
– Ray Bradbury

"Learning to let go should be learned before learning to get. Life should be touched, not strangled. You've got to relax, let it happen at times, and at others move forward with it."
– Ray Bradbury

"There are those whose lives affect all others around them. Quietly touching one heart, who in turn, touches another. Reaching out to ends further than they would ever know."
– William Bradfield

"Respect your fellow human being, treat them fairly, disagree with them honestly, enjoy their friendship, explore your thoughts about one another candidly, work together for a common goal and help one another achieve it."
– Bill Bradley

"Striving for excellence motivates you; striving for perfection is demoralizing."
– Harriet Braiker

"Envisioning the end is enough to put the means in motion"
– Dorothea Brande

"There is overwhelming evidence that the higher the level of self-esteem, the more likely one will be to treat others with respect, kindness, and generosity."
– Nathanial Branden

"You couldn't erase the past. You couldn't even change it. But sometimes life offered you the opportunity to put it right."
– Ann Brashares

"There is no effect more disproportionate to its cause than the happiness bestowed by a small compliment."
– Robert Brault

"Enjoy the little things, for one day you may look back and realize they were the big things."
– Robert Brault

"What we find in a soulmate is not something wild to tame but something wild to run with."
– Robert Brault

"Tue world needs dreamers and the world needs doers. But above all, the world needs dreamers who do."
– Sarah Ban Breathnach

"Making the best of ourselves is the reason we were born, but it takes patience and perseverance."
– Sarah Ban Breathnach

"If I could I would always work in silence and obscurity, and let my efforts be known by their results."
– Emily Bronte

"Nothing is so soothing to our self esteem as to find our bad traits in our forebears. It seems to absolve us."
– Van Wyck Brooks

"There is but one ocean though its coves have many names; a single sea of atmosphere with no coves at all; the miracle of soil, alive and giving life, lying thin on the only Earth, for which there is no spare."
– David Brower,

"You are a phenomenon no less magical than any possibility. You could just as easily have been born a thousand years ago in what is now Thailand, or hatched yesterday as a dragonfly. Why not live as extravagantly as the odds are preposterous you showed up like this?"
– D.W. Brown

"Live so that when your children think of fairness and integrity, they think of you."
– H. Jackson Brown, Jr.

"Remember that everyone you meet is afraid of something, loves something, and has lost something."
– H. Jackson Brown, Jr.

"Our character is what we do when we think no one is looking."
– H. Jackson Brown, Jr.

"Nothing is more expensive than a missed opportunity."
– H. Jackson Brown, Jr.

"If you set goals and go after them with all the determination you can muster, your gifts will take you places that will amaze you."
– Les Brown

"Wanting something is not enough. You must hunger for it. Your motivation must be absolutely compelling in order to overcome the obstacles that will invariably come your way."
– Les Brown

"You need to make a commitment, and once you make it, then life will give you some answers."
– Les Brown

"A life of reaction is a life of slavery, intellectually and spiritually. One must fight for a life of action, not reaction."
– Rita Mae Brown

"Light tomorrow with today."
– Elizabeth Barrett Browning

"Music enters our bodies, commandeering the pulse in our veins, and reminds us that pleasure isn't a matter of feeling good but of feeling more alive."
– Holly Brubach

"Destiny is not a matter of chance, it is a matter of choice; it is not a thing to be waited for, it is a thing to be achieved."
– William Jennings Bryan

"I don't wait for moods. You accomplish nothing if you do that. Your mind must know it has got to get down to work."
– Pearl S. Buck

"Every trial endured and weathered in the right spirit makes a soul nobler and stronger than it was before."
– James Buckham

"As an irrigator guides water to his fields, as an archer aims an arrow, as a carpenter carves wood, the wise shape their lives."
– Gautama Buddha

"Holding onto anger is like drinking poison and expecting the other person do die."
– Gautama Buddha

"The heart is like a garden. It can grow compassion or fear, resentment or love. What seeds will you plant there?"
– Gautama Buddha

"Three things cannot be long hidden: the sun, the moon, and the truth."
– Gautama Buddha

"The eating of meat extinguishes the seed of great compassion."

– Gautama Buddha

"Just as a candle cannot burn without fire, men cannot live without a spiritual life."

– Gautama Buddha

"The secret of health for both mind and body is not to mourn for the past, not to worry about the future, or not to anticipate troubles, but to live in the present moment wisely and earnestly."

– Gautama Buddha

"There are two mistakes one can make along the road to truth...not going all the way, and not starting."

– Gautama Buddha

"May fear and dread not conquer me."

– Gautama Buddha

"The life I touch for good or ill will touch another life, and that in turn another, until who knows where the trembling stops or in what far place my touch will be felt."

– Frederick Buechner

"The problem with the world is that the intelligent people are full of doubts while the stupid ones are full of confidence."

– Charles Bukowski

"People with no morals often considered themselves more free, but mostly they lacked the ability to feel or love."

– Charles Bukowski

"A good heart is better than all the heads in the world."
— Edward G. Bulwer-Lytton

"When a person is down in the world, an ounce of help is better than a pound of preaching."
— Edward G. Bulwer-Lytton

"Mindfulness can be summed up in two words: pay attention. Once you notice what you're doing, you have the power to change it."
— Michelle Burford

"In prosperity prepare for a change; in adversity hope for one."
— James Burgh

"Acknowledging a person for the good that they do is good, but not as good as committing to do that same good yourself."
— Melanie E. Burgos

"Nobody made a greater mistake than the person who did nothing, because they thought that they could only do a little."
— Edmund Burke

"We don't grow unless we take risks. Any successful company is riddled with failures."
— James E. Burke

"Only I can change my life. No one can do it for me."
— Carol Burnett

"I pick my favorite quotation and store them in my mind as ready armor, offensive or defensive, amid the struggle of this turbulent existence."
– Robert Burns

"The lure of the distant and the difficult is deceptive. The great opportunity is where you are."
– John Burroughs

"A man can get discouraged many times, but he is not a failure until he begins to blame somebody else and stops trying."
– John Burroughs

"Every man has inside himself a parasitic being who is acting not at all to his advantage."
– William S. Burroughs

"Love? What is it? Most natural pain killer that there is. Love."
– William S. Burroughs

"Love abhors waste, especially waste of human potential."
– Leo Buscaglia

"Love yourself, accept yourself, and be good to yourself, because without you the rest of us are without a source of many wonderful things."
– Leo Buscaglia

"Life is a great and wondrous mystery, and the only thing we know that we have for sure is what is right here right now. Don't miss it."
– Leo Buscaglia

"Life is uncharted territory. It reveals its story one moment at a time."
– Leo Buscaglia

"There are scores of people waiting for someone just like us to come along; people who will appreciate our compassion, our encouragement, who will need our unique talents. Someone who will live a happier life merely because we took the time to share what we had to give."
– Leo Buscaglia

"The question, 'Who am I?' is not a philosophical football meant to be kicked around coffeehouses by pseudo-intellectuals. It's a real-life question. Nothing is more important and more relevant than to know who you are."
– Chris Butler

"Every man's work, whether it be literature or music or pictures or architecture or anything else, is always a portrait of himself."
– Samuel Butler

"Life is not an exact science, it is an art."
– Samuel Butler

"The purpose of life is a life of purpose."
– Robert Byrne

# C

"We carry our homes within us which enables us to fly."

– John Cage

"It is by going down into the abyss that we recover the treasures of life. Where you stumble, there lies your treasure."

– Joseph Campbell

"People say that what we're all seeking is a meaning for life. I don't think that's what we're really seeking. I think that what we're seeking is an experience of being alive, so that our life experiences on the purely physical plane will have resonances with our own innermost

being and reality, so that we actually feel the rapture of being alive."
– Joseph Campbell

"Love is a friendship set to music."
– Joseph Campbell

"Opportunities to find deeper powers within ourselves come when life seems most challenging."
– Joseph Campbell

"Life has no meaning. Each of us has meaning and we can bring it to life. It is a waste to be asking the question when you are the answer."
– Joseph Campbell

"I don't believe people are looking for the meaning of life as much as they are looking for the experience of being alive."
– Joseph Campbell

"In the depths of winter I finally learned there was in me an invincible summer."
– Albert Camus

"If there is a sin against life, it consists perhaps not so much in despairing of life as in hoping for another life and in eluding the implacable grandeur of this life."
– Albert Camus

"Do not wait for the last judgment. It takes place every day."
– Albert Camus

"It takes twenty years to become an overnight success."
– Eddie Cantor

"The current extinction event is due to human activity, paving the planet, creating pollution, many of the things that we are doing today. The Earth might well lose half of its species in our lifetime. We want to know which ones deserve the highest priority for conservation."

–Bradley Cardinale

"Trying to be happy by accumulating possessions is like trying to satisfy hunger by taping sandwiches all over your body."

– George Carlin

"Since childhood is a time when kids prepare to be grown-ups, I think it makes a lot of sense to completely traumatize your children. Gets 'em ready for the real world."

– George Carlin

"People are wonderful one at a time. Each one of them has an entire hologram of the universe somewhere within them."

– George Carlin

"The real reason that we can't have the Ten Commandments in a courthouse: You cannot post 'Thou shalt not steal,' 'Thou shalt not commit adultery,' and 'Thou shalt not lie' in a building full of lawyers, judges, and politicians. It creates a hostile work environment."

– George Carlin

"I consider a goal as a journey rather than a destination. And each year I set a new goal."

– Curtis Carlson

"Most of the important things in the world have been accomplished by people who have kept on trying when there seemed to be no hope at all."
– Dale Carnegie

"We are evaluated and classified by these four contacts: what we do, how we look, what we say, and how we say it."
– Dale Carnegie

"If you want to conquer fear don't sit home and think about it. Go out and get busy."
– Dale Carnegie

"All life is a chance. So take it!"
– Dale Carnegie

"It is the greatest truth of our age: Information is not knowledge."
– Caleb Carr

"Your job is not to figure out how it's going to happen for you, it's opening a door in your head, and when the door opens in real life, just walk through it."
– Jim Carrey

"If you've got a talent, protect it."
– Jim Carrey

"One day Alice came to a fork in the road and saw a Cheshire cat in a tree. Which road do I take? she asked. Where do you want to go? was his response. I don't know, Alice answered. Then, said the cat, it doesn't matter."
– Lewis Carroll

"Will you, won't you, will you, won't you, will you join the dance?"
– Lewis Carroll

"If I had influence with the good fairy, I would ask that her gift to each child be a sense of wonder so indestructible that it would last throughout life."
– Rachel Carson

"For the first time in the history of the world, every human being is now subjected to contact with dangerous chemicals, from the moment of conception until death."
– Rachel Carson

"The more clearly we can focus our attention on the wonders and realities of the universe about us, the less taste we shall have for destruction."
– Rachel Carson

"How far you go in life depends on your being tender with the young, compassionate with the aged, sympathetic with the striving, and tolerant of the weak and the strong, because someday in your life, you will have been all of these."
– George Washington Carver

"The best time to plant an oak tree was twenty-five years ago. The second best time is today."
– James Carville

"It takes courage for people to listen to their own goodness and act on it."
– Pablo Casals

"In some strange way, any new fact or insight that I may have found has not seemed to me as a 'discovery' of mine, but rather something that had always been there and that I had chanced to pick up."
– Subrahmanijan Chandrasekhar

"The most courageous act is still to think for yourself. Aloud."
– Gabrielle Coco Chanel

"Elegance is not the prerogative of those who have just escaped from adolescence, but of those who have already taken possession of their future."
– Gabrielle Coco Chanel

"To live content with small means; to seek elegance rather than luxury, and refinement rather than fashion; to be worthy, not respectable, and wealthy, not rich; to listen to stars and birds, babes and sages with open heart; to study hard, to think quietly, act frankly, talk gently, await occasions, hurry never; in a word, to let the spiritual, unbidden and unconscious, grow up through the common – this is my symphony."
– William Channing

"We think too much and feel too little. More than machinery, we need humanity. More than cleverness, we need kindness and gentleness."
– Charlie Chaplin

"We think too much and feel too little. More than machinery, we need humanity. More than cleverness, we need kindness and gentleness."
– Charlie Chaplin

"What is a soul? It's like electricity - we don't really know what it is, but it's a force that can light a room."
— Ray Charles

"To understand is to forgive, even oneself."
— Alexander Chase

"It's amazing how people can get so excited about a rocket to the moon and not give a damn about smog, oil leaks, the devastation of the environment with pesticides, hunger, disease. When the poor share some of the power that the affluent now monopolize, we will give a damn."
— Cesar Chavez

"If you wait for the perfect moment when all is safe and assured, it may never arrive. Mountains will not be climbed, races won, or lasting happiness achieved."
— Maurice Chefalier

"Knowledge is of no value unless you put it into practice."
— Anton Chekhov

"What helps luck is a habit of watching for opportunities, of having a patient but restless mind, of sacrificing one's ease or vanity, or uniting a love of detail to foresight, and of passing through hard times bravely and cheerfully."
— Charles Victor Cherbuliez

"Little, vicious minds abound with anger and revenge, and are incapable of feeling the pleasure of forgiving their enemies."
— Lord Chesterfield

"A man does not know what he is saying until he knows what he is not saying."
– Gilbert K Chesterton

"There are no uninteresting things, there are only uninterested people."
– Gilbert K. Chesterton

"Thousands of roads enter the great path of Tao. To find such a road means one has found one's Ding. Creating a masterpiece can be such a road, or religion, or a Koan, or even growing beans. But however small one's Ding may be, it always contains the huge inner storage of spiritual richness. It gives consecration to one's life, making its size unimportant. And making it invulnerable for any attacks. It will be a true life and it will earn a place in the annals of Heaven."
– I Ching

"When you begin to touch your heart or let your heart be touched, you begin to discover that it's bottomless, that it doesn't have any resolution, that this heart is huge, vast, and limitless. You begin to discover how much warmth and gentleness is there, as well as how much space."
– Pema Chodron

"It's said that when we die, the four elements – earth, air, fire and water – dissolve one by one, each into the other, and finally just dissolve into space. But while we're living, we share the energy that makes everything, from a blade of grass to an elephant, grow and live and then inevitably wear out and die. This energy, this life force, creates the whole world."
– Pema Chodron

"The point of public relations slogans like 'Support our troops' is that they don't mean anything. That's the whole point of good propaganda. You want to create a slogan that nobody's going to be against, and everybody's going to be for. Nobody knows what it means, because it doesn't mean anything. Its crucial value is that it diverts your attention from a question that does mean something: Do you support our policy? That's the one you're not allowed to talk about."
– Norm Chomsky

"All over the place, from the popular culture to the propaganda system, there is constant pressure to make people feel that they are helpless, that the only role they can have is to ratify decisions and to consume."
– Noam Chomsky

"The whole educational and professional system is a very elaborate filter, which just weeds out people who are too independent, and who think for themselves, and who don't know how to be submissive, and so on – because they're dysfunctional to the institutions."
– Noam Chomsky

"In the US, there is basically one party – the business party. It has two factions, called Democrats and Republicans, which are somewhat different but carry out variations on the same policies. By and large, I am opposed to those policies. As is most of the population."
– Noam Chomsky

"We have stopped for a moment to encounter each other, to meet, to love, to share. This is a precious moment but it is transient. It is a little parenthesis in eternity. If we share caring, lightheartedness, and love, we will create abundance and joy for each other. And then this moment will be worthwhile.

– Deepak Chopra

"If you want to reach a state of bliss, then go beyond your ego and the internal dialogue. Make a decision to relinquish the need to control, the need to be approved, and the need to judge."

– Deepak Chopra

"The web of life in our oceans is being pulled apart as top predators like tuna have crashed from overfishing; trawling for groundfish and scallops has scraped some areas of the ocean bottom clean like a parking lot; and pollution and nutrient-rich runoff have fed algae blooms and jellyfish population explosions, resulting in what one scientist calls 'the sliming of the oceans.'"

– Jon Christensen

"I like living. I have sometimes been wildly, despairingly, acutely miserable, racked with sorrow, but through it all I still know quite certainly that just to be alive is a grand thing."

– Agatha Christie

"Success is going from failure to failure without a loss of enthusiasm."

– Winston Churchill

"To improve is to change; to be perfect is to change often."

– Winston Churchill

"Make choices based on what gives you a sense of fulfillment, not fear."

– Pauline Rose Clance

"Life is change. Growth is optional. Choose wisely."
– Karen Kaiser Clark

"Conscience is the root of all true courage; if a man would be brave let him obey his conscience."
– James Freeman Clarke

"Inspiration is for amateurs. The rest of us just show up and get the work done. If you wait around for the clouds to part and a bolt of lightning to strike you in the brain, you're not going to make an awful lot of work."
– Chuck Close

"I'd rather be hated for who I am, than loved for who I am not."
– Kurt Cobain

"I'm not gay, although I wish I were, just to piss off the homophobes."
– Kurt Cobain

"I prefer to be crazy and happy rather than normal and bitter."
– Paulo Coelho

"Do not wait until the conditions are perfect to begin. Beginning makes the conditions perfect."
– Alan Cohen

"Follow your dreams, work hard, practice and persevere. Make sure you eat a variety of foods, get plenty of exercise and maintain a healthy lifestyle."
– Sasha Cohen

"The happiness of life… is made up of minute fractions – the little, soon-forgotten charities of a kiss, a smile, a kind look, a heartfelt compliment in the disguise

of playful raillery, and the countless infinitesimals of pleasurable thought and genial feeling."
– Samuel Taylor Coleridge

"As fast as each opportunity presents itself, use it! No matter how tiny an opportunity it may be, use it!"
– Robert Collier

"Start where you are. Distant fields always look greener, but opportunity lies right where you are. Take advantage of every opportunity of service."
– Robert J. Collier

"No one who deserves confidence ever solicits it."
– John Churton Collins

"Success doesn't come to you, you go to it."
– Marva Collins

"Determination and perseverance move the world; thinking that others will do it for you is a sure way to fail."
– Marva Collins

"Some walks you have to take alone."
– Suzanne Collins

"Times of general calamity and confusion have ever been production of the greatest minds. The purest ore is produced from the hottest furnace."
– Charles Caleb Colton

"We don't challenge kids in schools. We don't challenge them to think; we don't challenge them to create. We challenge them to get good enough grades to get into a good enough college."
– Bob Compton

"Our greatest glory consists not in never falling, but in rising every time we fall."
– Confucius

"Before you embark on a journey of revenge, dig two graves."
– Confucius

"Real knowledge is to know the extent of one's own ignorance."
– Confucius

"Creativity is inventing, experimenting, growing, taking risks, breaking rules, making mistakes, and having fun."
– Mary Lou Cook

"Anyone can dabble, but once you've made that commitment, your blood has that particular thing in it, and it's very hard for people to stop you."
– Bill Cosby

"You must speak straight so that your words may go as sunlight to our hearts."
– Coshise

"Whenever I give young people advice, I implore them not to take critics and their negativity to heart. There are many people who will try to stand in your way, even cut you off at the knees, but it is often more about them than about you. Learning this early on helped me believe in myself, even when some around me did not."
– Katie Couric

"Always in life an idea starts small, it is only a sapling idea, but the vines will come and they will try to choke your idea so it cannot grow and it will die and you will

never know you had a big idea, an idea so big it could have grown thirty meters through the dark canopy of leaves and touched the face of the sky."
– Bryce Courtenay

"If you realize you are only a violin, you can open yourself up to the world by playing your role in the concert."
– Jacques Yves Cousteau

"Free your heart from hatred – forgive. Free your mind from worries – most never happen. Live simply and appreciate what you have. Give more. Expect less."
– Stephen Covey

"Do not trust the cheering, for those persons would should as much if you and I were going to be hanged."
– Oliver Cromwell

"The greatest power is often simple patience."
– E Joseph Crossman

"There is as much risk in doing nothing as in doing something."
– Trammell Crow

"I admit that my visions can never mean to other men as much as they do to me. I do not regret this. All I ask is that my results should convince seekers after truth that there is beyond doubt something worthwhile seeking, attainable by methods more or less like mine. I do not want to father a flock, to be the fetish of fools and fanatics, or the founder of a faith whose followers are content to echo my opinions. I want each man to cut his own way through the jungle."
– Aleister Crowley

"So what if you bomb? You learn from it. You pick yourself up, try to figure out what went wrong and then move on, knowing you've given it your best shot."
– Billy Crystal

"People think being alone makes you lonely, but I don't think that's true. Being surrounded by the wrong people is the loneliest thing in the world."
– Kim Culbertson

"To be nobody-but-yourself – in a world which is doing its best, night and day, to make you everybody else – means to fight the hardest battle which any human being can fight; and never stop fighting."
– E.E. Cummings

"Life is not easy for any of us. But what of that? We must have perseverance and above all confidence in ourselves. We must believe that we are gifted for something, and that this thing, at whatever cost, must be attained."
– Marie Curie

"The fact is, that to do anything in the world worth doing, we must not stand back shivering and thinking of the cold and danger, but jump in and scramble through as well as we can."
– Robert Cushing

# D

"Above all, watch with glittering eyes the whole world around you, because the greatest secrets are always hidden in the most unlikely places. Those who don't believe in magic will never find it."
– Roald Dahl

"Each person has an ideal, a hope, a dream which represents the soul. We must give it to the warmth of love, the light of understanding, and the essence of encouragement."
– Colby Dorr Dam

"Never let your persistence and passion turn into stubbornness and ignorance."
– Anthony J. D'Angelo

"Focus 90% of your time on solutions and only 10% of your time on problems."
– Anthony J. D'Angelo

"I wish you the joy of a purposeful life. I wish you new worlds and the vision to see them. I wish you the decency and the nobility of which you are capable."
– Jonathan Myrick Daniels

"It is not the strongest of the species that survive, nor the most intelligent, but the one most responsive to change."
– Charles Darwin

"We're all just walking each other home."
– Ram Dass

"The shadow is the greatest teacher for how to come to the light."
– Ram Dass

"We need not think alike to love alike."
– Frances David

"Nature, by example, shows us anything worthwhile comes over time. Anything worthwhile grows methodically, building on a strong foundation. Develop a willingness to carry on despite roadblocks."
– Jaren L. Davis

"Truly man is the king of beasts, for his brutality exceeds theirs. We live by the death of others: we are burial places. I have from an early age abjured the use of meat, and the time will come when men such as I will

look on the murder of animals as they now look on the murder of men."
— Leonardo da Vinci

"Principles are for the development of a complete mind: study the science of art. Study the art of science. Develop your senses – especially learn how to see. Realize that everything connects to everything else."
— Leonardo da Vinci

"If you understood everything I said, you'd be me."
— Miles Davis

"I have found that when you are deeply troubled, there are things you get form the silent devoted companionship of a dog that you can get from no other source."
— Doris Day

"We plant seeds that will flower as results in our lives, so best to remove the weeds of anger, avarice, envy, and doubt, that peace and abundance may manifest for all."
— Dorothy Day

"We have all known the long loneliness and we have learned that the only solution is love and that love comes with community."
— Dorothy Day

"It is not given us to live lives of undisrupted calm, boredom, and mediocrity. It is given us to be edge-dwellers."
— Jay Deacon

"Dream as if you'll live forever. Live as if you'll die today."

– James Dean

"Poverty was the biggest motivating factor in my life."

– Jimmy Dean

"It is in the knowledge of the genuine conditions of our lives that we must draw our strength to live and our reasons for living."

– Simone de Beauvoir

"Be means of all created things, without exception, the divine assails us, penetrates us and moulds us. We imagined it as distant and inaccessible, whereas in fact we live steeped in its burning layers."

– Pierre Teilhard de Chardin

"You are not a human being in search of a spiritual experience. You are a spiritual being immersed in a human experience."

– Pierre Teilhard de Chardin

"The greatest foes, and whom we must chiefly combat, are within."

– Miguel De Cervantes

"Action makes more fortune than caution."

– Luc De Clapiers

"We are, each of us angels with only one wing; and we can only fly by embracing one another."

– Lucianno de Crescenzo

"Your goal should be out of reach but not out of sight."
– Anita DeFrantz

"You are the material itself of the Great Work."
– Grillot de Givry

"When we are unable to find tranquility within ourselves, it is useless to seek it elsewhere."
– Francois de La Rochefoucauld

"In the presence of some people we inevitably depart from ourselves: we are inaccurate, we say things we do not feel, and talk nonsense. When we get home we are conscious that we have made fools of ourselves. Never go near these people."
– Francois de La Rochefoucauld

"Courage consists, however, in agreeing to flee rather than live tranquilly and hypocritically in false refuges. Values, morals, homelands, religions, and these private certitudes that our vanity and our complacency bestow generously on us, have many deceptive sojourns as the world arranges for those who think they are standing straight and at ease, among stable things."
– Gilles Deleuze

"Happiness resides not in possessions, and not in gold, happiness dwells in the soul."
– Democritus

"If we only wanted to be happy it would be easy; but we want to be happier than other people, which is almost always difficult, since we think them happier than they are."
– Charles de Mondesquieu

"You can close your eyes to the things you don't want to see, but you can't close your heart to the things you don't want to feel."

– Johnny Depp

"We are all damaged in our own way. Nobody is perfect. I think we are all somewhat screwy, every single one of us."

– Johnny Depp

"Just keep moving forward, and don't give a shit about what anybody thinks. Do what you have to do, for you."

– Johnny Depp

"You'll be bothered from time to time by storms, fog, snow. When you are, think of those who went through it before you, and say to yourself, 'What they could do, I can do.'"

– Antoine de Saint Exupery

"I know but one freedom and that is the freedom of the mind."

– Antoine de Saint-Exupery

"If you want to build a ship, don't herd people together to collect wood and don't assign them tasks and work, but rather teach them to long for the endless immensity of the sea."

– Antoine de Saint-Exupery

"As for the future, your task is not to foresee it, but to enable it."

– Antoine de Saint-Exupery

"Defeat is a thing of weariness, of incoherence, of boredom."
– Antoine de Saint-Exupiry

"If you would be a real seeker after truth, it is necessary that at least once in your life you doubt, as far as possible, all things."
– Rene Descartes

"We should expect the best and the worst of mankind, as from the weather."
– Marquis De Vauvenargues

"As the body needs food to survive and grow, the soul needs love. Love instills a strength and vitality that even mother's milk cannot provide. All of us live and long for real love. We are born and die searching for such love. Children, love each other and unite in pure love."
– Mata Amritanandamayl "Amma" Devi

"No one is useless in this world who lightens the burdens of another."
– Charles Dickens

"Reflect upon your present blessings – of which every man has many – not on your past misfortunes, of which all man have some."
– Charles Dickens

"I never could have done what I have done without the habits of punctuality, order, and diligence, without the determination to concentrate myself on one subject at a time."
– Charles Dickens

"Whatever I have tried to do in life, I have tried with all my heart to do it well; whatever I have devoted myself to, I have devoted myself completely; in great aims and in small I have always thoroughly been in earnest."
– Charles Dickens

"Unable are the loved to die, for love is immortality."
– Emily Dickinson

"If I can stop one heart from breaking, I shall not live in vain; If I can ease one life the aching, or cool one pain, or help one fainting robin up to his nest again, I shall not live in vain."
– Emily Dickinson

"Unable are the loved to die, for love is immortality."
– Emily Dickinson

"We tell ourselves stories in order to live."
– Joan Didion

"I know there is strength in the difference between us. I know there is comfort, where we overlap."
– Ani DiFranco

"How we spend our days is, of course, how we spend our lives."
– Annie Dillard

"When you have a great and difficult task, something perhaps almost impossible, if you only work a little at a time, every day a little, suddenly the work will finish itself."
– Isak Dinesen

"Through perseverance many people win success out of what seemed destined to be certain failure."

– Benjamin Disraeli

"Patience is a necessary ingredient of genius."

– Benjamin Disraeli

"One of the hardest things in this world is to admit you are wrong. And nothing is more helpful in resolving a situation than its frank admission."

– Benjamin Disraeli

"We are not creatures of circumstance; we are creators of circumstance."

– Benjamin Disraeli

"Nurture your mind with great thoughts, for you will never go any higher than what you think."

– Banjamin Disraeli

"You can't expect anyone to clean up the dirt left behind by bitterness inside your own mind."

– Dodinsky

"To strengthen the muscles of your heart, the best exercise is lifting someone else's spirit whenever you can."

– Dodinsky

"Get over the idea that only children should spend their time in study. Be a student so long you still have something to learn, and this will mean all your life."

– Henry L. Doherty

"Love so joyfully and freely given can never be taken away. It is never truly gone."

– Cameron Dokey

"Be thine own palace, or the world's thy jail."
– John Donne

"Plants have always been used by shamans to enter the inner realm."
– Donovan

"Dedicate some of your life to others. Your dedication will not be a sacrifice. It will be an exhilarating experience because it is an intense effort applied toward a meaningful end."
– Thomas Dooley

"Originality and feeling of one's own dignity are achieved only through work and struggle."
– Fyodor Dostoevsky

"Love the world with an all-embracing love. Love the animals; God has given them the rudiments of thought and joy untroubled. Do not trouble them, do not harass them, do not deprive them of their happiness, do not work against God's intent. Man, do not pride yourself on your superiority to them, for they are without sin, and you with your greatness defile the earth."
– Fyodor Dostoyevsky

"Where justice is denied, where poverty is enforced, where ignorance prevails, and where any one class is made to feel that society is an organized conspiracy to oppress, rob, and degrade them, neither persons nor property will be safe."
– Frederick Douglass

"If there is no struggle, there is no progress. Those who profess to favor freedom, and yet deprecate agitation, are people who want rain without thunder and lightning. They want the ocean without the roar of its

many waters. Power concedes nothing without a demand. It never did and it never will."
– Frederick Douglass

"It's okay to look back at the past. Just don't stare."
– Benjamin Dover

"It has long been an axiom of mine that the little things are infinitely the most important."
– Arthur Conan Doyle

"When you have eliminated all which is impossible, then whatever remains, however improbable, must be the truth."
– Arthur Conan Doyle

"My greatest strength as a consultant is to be ignorant and ask a few questions."
– Peter F. Drucker

"The entrepreneur always searches for change, responds to it, and exploits it as an opportunity."
– Peter F. Drucker

"Start with what is right rather than what is acceptable."
– Peter F. Drucker

"Unless commitment is made, there are only promises and hopes, but no plans."
– Peter F. Drucker

"Start with what is right rather than what is acceptable."
– Peter F. Drucker

"When your views on the world and your intellect are being challenged and you begin to feel uncomfortable because of a contradiction you've detected that is threatening your current model of the world… pay attention. You are about to learn something."

– William H. Drury, Jr.

"We are each gifted in a unique and important way. It is our privilege and our adventure to discover our own special light."

– Evelyn Mary Dunbar

"We are each gifted in a unique and important way. It is our privilege and our adventure to discover our own special light."

– Evelyn Mary Dunbar

"Good, better, best. Never let it rest. Until your good is better and your better is best."

– Tim Duncan

"Forget mistakes. Forget failure. Forget everything except what you're going to do now and do it. Today is your lucky day."

– Will Durant

"If I had listened to everyone who told me no, I'd never have gotten anything accomplished. When I really believe in something and someone says, 'You can't do it,' it just spurs me on."

– Shelley Duvall

"Be miserable. Or motivate yourself. Whatever has to be done, it's always your choice."

– Wayne Dyer

"Everything in the universe has a purpose. Indeed, the invisible intelligence that flows through everything in a purposeful fashion is also flowing through you."
– Wayne Dyer

"How people treat you is their karma; how you react is yours."
– Wayne Dyer

"What's money? A man is a success if he gets up in the morning and goes to bed at night and in between does what he wants to do."
– Bob Dylan

# E

"There is hope if people will begin to awaken that spiritual part of themselves, that heartfelt knowledge that we are caretakers of this planet."
– Brooke Medicine Eagle

"Without some kind of desire or attraction we would not be roused to the labor of knowledge in the first place; but to know truly, we must also seek to surmount the snares and ruses of desire as best we can. We must not try to disfigure what we strive to know through fantasy, or reduce the object of knowledge to a narcissistic image of ourselves."
– Terry Eagleton

"True civilizations do not hold predawn power breakfasts."
– Terry Eagleton

"Trouble in the air is very rare. It is hitting the ground that causes it."
– Amelia Earhart

"The most effective way to do it, is to do it."
– Amelia Earhart

"I hope for your help to explore and protect the wild ocean in ways that will restore the health and, in so doing, secure hope for humankind. Health to the ocean means health for us."
– Sylvia Earle

"There exists only the present instant... a Now which always and without end is itself new. There is no yesterday nor any tomorrow, but only Now, as it was a thousand years ago and as it will be a thousand years hence."
– Meister Eckhart

"The outward man is the swinging door; the inner man is the still hinge."
– Meister Eckhart

"The eye through which I see God is the same eye through which God sees me; my eye and God's eye are one eye, one seeing, one knowing, one love."
– Meister Eckhart

"It's time for greatness – not for greed. It's a time for idealism – not ideology. It is a time not just for compassionate words, but compassionate action."
– Marian Wright Edelman

"Opportunity is missed by most people because it comes dressed in overalls and looks like work."
– Thomas A. Edison

"Genius is one percent inspiration and ninety-nine percent perspiration."
– Thomas A. Edison

"There is far more opportunity than there is ability."
– Thomas A. Edison

"What you are will show in what you do."
– Thomas A. Edison

"When you have exhausted all possibilities, remember this: you haven't."
– Thomas A. Edison

"To dream anything that you want to dream. That's the beauty of the human mind. To do anything that you want to do. That is the strength of the human will. To trust yourself to test your limits. That is the courage to succeed."
– Bernard Edmonds

"The thing that impresses me the most about Americas is the way parents obey their children."
– Prince Edward, Duke of Windsor

"Thoughts lead on to purposes; purposes go forth in action; actions form habits; habits decide character; and character fixes our destiny."
– Tyron Edwards

"Right actions in the future are the best apologies for bad actions in the past."
– Tyron Edwards

"A knowledge of the existence of something we cannot penetrate, of the manifestations of the profoundest reason and the most radiant beauty, which are only accessible to our reason in their most elementary forms — it is this knowledge and this emotion that constitute the truly religious attitude; in this sense, and in this alone, I am a deeply religious man."
– Albert Einstein

"Out of clutter, find simplicity."
– Albert Einstein

"Everyone should be respected as an individual, but no one idolized."
– Albert Einstein

"Imagination is more important thán knowledge. For knowledge is limited to all we now know and understand, while imagination embraces the entire world, and all there ever will be to know and understand."
– Albert Einstein

"Any fool can make things bigger, more complex, and more violent. It takes a touch of genius-and a lot of courage-to move in the opposite direction."
– Albert Einstein

"The only thing that interferes with my learning is my education."
– Albert Einstein

"It is a miracle that curiosity survives formal education."
– Albert Einstein

"Look deep into nature, and then you will understand everything better."
– Albert Einstein

"True religion is real living; living with all one's soul, with all one's goodness and righteousness."
– Albert Einstein

"Great spirits have always found violent opposition from mediocre minds. The latter cannot understand it when a man does not thoughtlessly submit to hereditary prejudices but honestly and courageously uses his intelligence and fulfills the duty to express the result of his thoughts in clear form."
– Albert Einstein

"If you want your children to be intelligent, read them fairy tales. If you want them to be more intelligent, read them more fairy tales."
– Albert Einstein

"The basic laws of the Universe are simple, but because our senses are limited, we can't grasp them. There is a pattern in creation. Science is never finished because the human mind only uses a small portion of its capacity, and man's exploration of his world is also limited. If we look at this tree outside whose roots search beneath the pavement for water, or a flower which sends its sweet smell to the pollinating bees, or even our own selves and the inner forces that drive us to act, we can see that we all dance to a mysterious tune, and the piper who plays this melody from an inscrutable distance – whatever name we give him – Creative Force, or God – escapes all book knowledge."
– Albert Einstein

"The one who follows the crowd will usually get no further than the crowd. The one who walks alone, is likely to find himself places no one has ever been.
– Albert Einstein

"Few is the number who think with their own minds and feel with their own hearts."
– Albert Einstein

"The one who follows the crowd will usually get no further than the crowd. The one who walks alone is likely to find himself in the places no one has ever been."
– Albert Einstein

"Everything is energy and that's all there is to it. Match the frequency of the reality you want and you cannot help but get that reality. It can be no other way. This is not philosophy. This is physics."
– Albert Einstein

"If the facts don't fit the theory, change the facts."
– Albert Einstein

"A man's ethical behavior should be based effectually on sympathy, education, and social ties and needs; no religious basis is necessary. Man would indeed be in a poor way if he had to be restrained by fear of punishment and hope of reward after death."
– Albert Einstein

"Perhaps the most basic challenge humanity faces is to awaken our capacity for collective knowing, and conscious action so that we can respond successfully to the immense social and ecological difficulties that now confront us."
– Duane Elgin

"For last year's words belong to last year's language, and next year's words await another voice. To make an end is to make a beginning."
– T.S. Eliot

"We shall not cease from exploration; and the end of all our exploring will be to arrive where we started, and know that place for the first time."
– T.S. Eliot

"What life have you if you have not life together? There is no life that is not in community."
– T.S. Eliot

"Only those who will risk going too far can possibly find out how far they can go."
– T. S. Eliot

"We shall not cease from exploration, and the end of all our exploring will be to arrive where we started and know the place for the first time."
– TS Eliot

"You are the music, whilst the music lasts."
– TS Eliot

"Wear a smile and have friends; wear a scowl and have wrinkles. What do we live for if not to make the world less difficult for each other?"
– George Eliot

"History shows us that people who end up changing the world are always nuts, until they are right and then they are genius."
– John Elliot

"Perseverance is not a long race; it is many short races after one another."

– Walter Elliott

"No matter what sort of adversity or challenge you might face, you can always believe that, with hope, it can be conquered and, in the end, you will be stronger for it."

– Brooke Ellison

"Don't try to guide someone with your words, encourage the awakening of their spirit through your actions."

– Garnet Emerald

"When a resolute young fellow steps up to the great bully, the world, and takes him boldly by the beard, he is often surprised to find it comes off in his hand, and that it was only tied on to scare away the timid adventures."

– Ralph Waldo Emerson

"There is no beautifier of complexion, or form, or behavior, like the wish to scatter joy and not pain around us."

– Ralph Waldo Emerson

"Be yourself; no base imitator of another, but your best self. There is something which you can do better than another. Listen to the inward voice and bravely obey that. Do the things at which you are great, not what you were never made for."

– Ralph Waldo Emerson

"What lies behind us and what lies before us are tiny matters compared to what lies within us. And when we bring what is within out into the world, miracles happen."

– Ralph Waldo Emerson

"None of us will ever accomplish anything excellent or commanding except when he listens to this whisper which is heard by him alone."

– Ralph Waldo Emerson

"In art the hand can never execute anything higher than the heart can inspire."

– Ralph Waldo Emerson

"Do not be too timid and squeamish about your actions. All life is an experiment. The more experiments you make the better. What if they are a little coarse, and you may get your coat soiled or torn? What if you do fail, and get fairly rolled in the dirt once or twice. Up again, you shall never be so afraid of a tumble."

– Ralph Waldo Emerson

"Don't waste life in doubts and fears; spend yourself on the work before you, well assured that the right performance of this hour's duties will be the best preparation for the hours and ages that will follow it."

– Ralph Waldo Emerson

"Enthusiasm is the mother of effort, and without it nothing great was ever achieved."

– Ralph Waldo Emerson

"The best lightning rod for your own protection is your own spine."

– Ralph Waldo Emerson

"Make the most of yourself, for that is all there is for you."

– Ralph Waldo Emerson

"You have just dined, and however scrupulously the slaughterhouse is concealed in the graceful distance of miles, there is complicity."

– Ralph Waldo Emerson

"Don't be pushed by your problems, be led by your dreams."

– Ralph Waldo Emerson

"We aim above the mark to hit the mark."

– Ralph Waldo Emerson

"No one can cheat you out of ultimate success but yourself."

– Ralph Waldo Emerson

"People do not seem to realize that their opinion of the world is also a confession of character."

– Ralph Waldo Emerson

"Character is higher than intellect. A great soul will be strong to live as well as think."

– Ralph Waldo Emerson

"Finish each day and be done with it. You have done what you could. Some blunders and absurdities no doubt crept in; forget them as soon as you can. Tomorrow is a new day; begin it well and serenely and with too high a spirit to be encumbered with your old nonsense."

– Ralph Waldo Emerson

"People seem not to see that their opinion of the world is also a confession of character."
– Ralph Waldo Emerson

"Whatever course you decide upon, there is always someone to tell you that you are wrong. There are always difficulties arising which tempt you to believe that your critics are right. To map out a course of action and follow it to an end requires courage."
– Ralph Waldo Emerson

"Do not go where the path may lead; go instead where there is no path and leave a trail."
– Ralph Waldo Emerson

"Most of the shadows of this life are caused by standing in one's own sunshine."
– Ralph Waldo Emerson

"Adopt the pace of nature: her secret is patience."
– Ralph Waldo Emerson

"Genius always finds itself a century too early."
– Ralph Waldo Emerson

"Our being is descending into us from we know not whence."
– Ralph Waldo Emerson

"Man is a stream whose source is hidden."
– Ralph Waldo Emerson

"When it is dark enough, you can see the stars."
– Ralph Waldo Emerson

"Whatever course you decide upon, there is always someone to tell you that you are wrong. There are always difficulties arising which tempt you to believe that your critics are right. To map out a course of action and follow it to an end requires courage."

– Ralph Waldo Emerson

"What you do speaks so loud that I cannot hear what you say."

– Ralph Waldo Emerson

"And those men took me thence, and led me up on to the third heaven, and placed me there; and I looked downwards, and saw the produce of these places, such as has never been known for goodness. And I saw all the sweet-flowering trees and beheld their fruits, which were sweet-smelling, and all the foods borne by them bubbling with fragrant exhalation. And in the midst of the trees that of life, in that place whereon the Lord rests, when he goes up into paradise; and this tree is of ineffable goodness and fragrance, and adorned more than every existing thing; and on all sides it is in form gold-looking and vermilion and fire-like and covers all, and it has produce from all fruits. Its root is in the garden at the earth's end. And paradise is between corruptibility and incorruptibility. And two springs come out which send forth honey and milk, and their springs send forth oil and wine, and they separate into four parts, and go round with quiet course, and go down into the Paradise of Eden, between corruptibility and incorruptibility."

– 2 Enoch 8:1-6

"Do not spoil what you have by desiring what you have not; but remember that what you now have was once among the things you only hoped for."

– Epictetus

"When we are offended at any man's fault, turn to yourself and study your own failings. Then you will forget your anger."
– Epictetus

"If you would be good, first believe that you are bad."
– Epictetus

"On the occasion of every misfortune that befalls you, remember to inquire what power you have for turning this event to use."
– Epictetus

"Unremarkable lives are held captive by a fear of not looking capable. Accept that you are a perpetual beginner, not helpless or irresponsible, but willing to admit you don't have all the answers. Admitting weakness is strength."
– Epictetus

"Give light, and the darkness will disappear of itself."
– Desiderius Erasmus

"The key to success is to keep growing in all areas of life - mental, emotional, spiritual, as well as physical."
– Julius Erving

"I do not have superior intelligence or faultless looks. I do not captivate a room or run a mile in under six minutes. I only succeeded because I was still working after everyone else went to sleep."
– Greg Evans

"I have never been contained except I made the prison."
– Mary Evans

"There are some people who live in a dream world, and there are some who face reality; and then there are those who turn one into the other."

– Douglas Everett

"Hard work spotlights the character of people: some turn up their sleeves, some turn up their noses, and some don't turn up at all."

– Sam Ewing

# F

"Listening to someone talk isn't at all like listening to their words played over on a machine. What you hear when you have a face before you is never what you hear when you have before you a winding tape."
– Oriana Fallaci

"You don't have to accept the invitation to get angry. Instead, practice forgiveness, empathy, and encouragement."
– Dan Fallon

"Sometimes people hold a core belief that is very strong. When they are presented with evidence that works against that belief, the new evidence cannot be accepted. It would create a feeling that is extremely

uncomfortable, called cognitive dissonance. And because it is so important to protect the core belief, they will rationalize, ignore, and even deny anything that doesn't fit in with the core belief."
    – Frantz Fanon

"Relationships of trust depend on our willingness to look not only to our own interests, but also the interests of others."
    – Peter Farquharson

"When my horse is running good, I don't stop to give him sugar."
    – William Faulkner

"Always dream and shoot higher than you know you can do. Do not bother just to be better than your contemporaries or predecessors. Try to be better than yourself."
    – William Faulkner

"Rise above the storm and you will find the sunshine."
    – Mario Fernandez

"Start off everyday with a simple smile and get it over with."
    – W. C. Fields

"So what will define greatness for your generation? I believe it is to use the knowledge that you have earned here to find ways, not only to connect to computers, but to connect to people; not only to bridge gaps in science, but to bridge gaps between cultures; not only to use numbers and formulas to create, but to use words to

lead, and in the process, to close the canyon between ignorance and understanding."
– Carly Fiorina

"Find life experiences and swallow them whole. Travel. Meet many people. Go down some dead ends and explore dark alleys. Try everything. Exhaust yourself in the glorious pursuit of life."
– Lawrence K. Fish

"The uncommitted life isn't worth living."
– Marshall Fishwick

"Just don't give up trying to do what you really want to do. Where there is love and inspiration, I don't think you can go wrong."
– Ella Fitzgerald

"For what it's worth: it's never too late or, in my case, too early to be whoever you want to be. There's no time limit, stop whenever you want. You can change or stay the same, there are no rules to this thing. We can make the best or the worst of it. I hope you make the best of it. And I hope you see things that startle you. I hope you feel things you never felt before. I hope you meet people with a different point of view. I hope you live a life you're proud of. If you find that you're not, I hope you have the courage to start all over again."
– F. Scott Fitzgerald

"It was only a sunny smile, and little it cost in the giving, but like morning light it scattered the night and made the day worth living."
– F. Scott Fitzgerald

"The only reason some people get lost in thought is because it's unfamiliar territory."

— Paul Fix

"This mind-and-body is the vessel of my life. I want to know it with the same organic immersion that sets a snow goose flying ten thousand miles every winter and spring."

— Paul R. Fleischman

"You don't get harmony when everybody sings the same note."

— Doug Floyd

"Victory is a thing of the will."

— Ferdinand Foch

"The most powerful weapon on earth is the human soul on fire."

— Ferdinand Foch

"Too many people overvalue what they are not and undervalue what they are."

— Malcolm S. Forbes

"The question "Who ought to be boss?" is like as "Who ought to be the tenor in the quartet?" Obviously, the man who can sing tenor."

— Henry Ford

"Always hold your head up, but be careful to keep your nose at a friendly level."

— Max L. Forman

"I suggest that the only books that influence us are those for which we are ready, and which have gone a little farther down our particular path than we have yet got ourselves."
– E. M. Forster

"If you could only love enough, you could be the most powerful person in the world."
– Emmet Fox

"An act of violence against nature should be judged as severely as that against society or another person. The turning over of a stone, the unnecessary felling of a tree, or the slaughter of an animal is a crime to be weighed in judgment against the wants and needs of the person and the values of his society."
– Michael J. Fox

"Being vegan is your statement that you reject violence to other sentient beings, to yourself, and to the environment, on which all sentient beings depend."
– Gary L. Francione

"Think of all the beauty still left around you and be happy."
– Anne Frank

"In spite of everything, I still believe that people are really good at heart. I simply can't build up my hopes on a foundation consisting of confusion, misery, and death."
– Anne Frank

"Our attitude towards what has happened to us in life is the important thing to recognize. Once hopeless, my life is now hope-full, but it did not happen overnight. The last of human freedoms, to choose one's attitude in

any given set of circumstances, is to choose one's own way."
— Viktor Frankl

"Between stimulus and response there is a space. In that space is our power to choose our response. In our response lies our growth and our freedom."
— Viktor E. Frankl

"Either write something worth reading, or do something worth writing."
— Benjamin Franklin

"Plough deep while sluggards sleep."
— Benjamin Franklin

"If passion drives you, let reason hold the reins."
— Benjamin Franklin

"Do not anticipate trouble, or worry about what may never happen. Keep in the sunlight."
— Benjamin Franklin

"Well done is better than well said."
— Benjamin Franklin

"Who is more foolish, the child afraid of the dark or the man afraid of the light?"
— Maurice Freehill

"The awful wrongs and sufferings forced upon the innocent, helpless, faithful animal race form the blackest chapter in the whole world's history."
— Edward Freeman

"We must stop constantly fighting for human rights and equal justice in an unjust system, and start building a society where equal rights are an integral part of the design."

– Jacque Fresco

"I was asked once, 'You're a smart man. Why aren't you rich?' I replied, 'You're a rich man. Why aren't you smart?'"

– Jacque Fresco

"Love and work are the cornerstones of our humanness."

– Sigmund Freud

"If you limit your choices only to what seems possible or reasonable, you disconnect yourself from what you truly want, and all that is left is compromise."

– Robert Fritz

"The quest for certainty blocks the search for meaning. Uncertainty is the very condition to impel man to unfold his powers."

– Erich Fromm

"Who will tell whether one happy moment of love or the joy of breathing or walking on a bright morning and smelling the fresh air, is not worth all the suffering and effort which life implies."

– Erich Fromm

"People who do not see their choices do not believe they have choices. They tend to respond automatically, blindly influenced by their circumstances and conditioning. Mindfulness, by helping us notice our

impulses before we act, gives us the opportunity to decide whether to act and how to act."
– Gil Fronsdal

"Fake friends are no different than shadows, they stick around during the brightest moments, but disappear during your darkest hours. No thanks! Be genuine or step off."
– Freelee Frugivore

"Don't worry that children never listen to you; worry that they are always watching you."
– Robert Fulghum

"We should do away with the absolutely specious notion that everybody has to earn a living. It is a fact today that one in ten thousand of us can make a technological breakthrough capable of supporting all the rest. The youth of today are absolutely right in recognizing this nonsense of earning a living. We keep inventing jobs because of this false idea that everybody has to be employed at some kind of drudgery because, according to Malthusian Darwinian theory he must justify his right to exist. So we have inspectors of inspectors and people making instruments for inspectors to inspect inspectors. The true business of people should be to go back to school and think about whatever it was they were thinking about before somebody came along and told them they had to earn a living."
– Richard Buckminster Fuller

"If I ran a school, I'd give the average grade to the ones who gave me all the right answers, for being good parrots. I'd give the top grades to those who made a lot

of mistakes and told me about them, and then told me what they learned from them."
– Richard Buckminster Fuller

"There is nothing in a caterpillar that tells you it's going to be a butterfly."
– Richard Buckminster Fuller

"We never know the worth of water till the well is dry."
– Thomas Fuller

"Unless you have some goals, I don't think there's any way to get above the pack. My vision was always well beyond what I had any reason to expect."
– John Fuqua

"Those who make compassion an essential part of their lives find the joy of life. Kindness deepens the spirit and produces rewards that cannot be completely explained in words. It is an experience more powerful than words. To become acquainted with kindness one must be prepared to learn new things and feel new feelings. Kindness is more than a philosophy of the mind. It is a philosophy of the spirit."
– Robert J. Furey

# G

"The one thing that you have that nobody else has is you. Your voice, your mind, your story, your vision. So write and draw and build and play and dance and live as only you can."
– Neil Gaiman

"If all else fails, immortality can always be assured by a spectacular error."
– John Kenneth Galbraith

"I do not believe that the same God who has endowed us with sense, reason, and intellect has intended us to forgo their use."
– Galileo Galilei

"The burned hand teaches best. After that advice about fire goes to the heart."
– Gandalf

"In the attitude of silence the soul finds the path in a clearer light, and what is elusive and deceptive resolves itself into crystal clearness."
– Mahatma Gandhi

"Faith must be enforced by reason... when faith becomes blind it dies."
– Mohandas Karamchand Gandhi

"Freedom is never dear at any price. It is the breath of life. What would a man not pay for living?"
– Mohandas Karamchand Gandhi

"It is the quality of our work which will please God and not the quantity."
– Mohandas Karamchand Gandhi

"A small body of determined spirits fired by an unquenchable faith in their mission can alter the course of history."
– Mohandas Karamchand Gandhi

"Constant development is the law of life, and a man who always tries to maintain his dogmas in order to appear consistent drives himself into a false position."
– Mohandas Karamchand Gandhi

"To believe in something, and not to live it, is dishonest."
– Mohandas Karamchand Gandhi

"The greatness of a nation can be judged by the way its animals are treated."
— Mohandas Karamchand Gandhi

"Man's nature is not essentially evil. Brute nature has been known to yield to the influence of love. You must never despair of human nature."
— Mohandas Karamchand Gandhi

"The difference between what we do and what we are capable of doing would suffice to solve most of the world's problems."
— Mohandas Karamchand Gandhi

"I suppose leadership at one time meant muscles; but today it means getting along with people."
— Mohandas Karamchand Gandhi

"Satisfaction lies in the effort, not in the attainment; full effort is full victory."
— Mohandas Karamchand Gandhi

"One of the reasons mature people stop learning is that they become less and less willing to risk failure."
— John W. Gardner

"Values provide perspective in the best of times and worst."
— Charles A. Garfield

"You have to find out what's right for you, so it's trial and error. You are going to be all right if you accept realistic goals for yourself."
— Teri Garr

"Life means to have something definite to do – a mission to be fulfilled – and in the measure in which we avoid setting our life to something, we make it empty. Human life, by its very nature, has to be dedicated to something."
– Jose Ortega y Gassett

"I was part of that strange race of people aptly described as spending their lives doing things they detest to make money they don't want to buy things they don't need to impress people they dislike."
– Emile Henry Gauvreau

"Every time you don't follow your inner guidance, you feel a loss of energy, loss of power, a sense of spiritual deadness."
– Shakti Gawain

"Trusting your intuition means tuning in as deeply as you can to the energy you feel, following that energy moment to moment, trusting that it will lead you where you want to go and bring you everything you desire."
– Shakti Gawain

"Problems are messages."
– Shakti Gawain

"If you cannot find peace within yourself, you will never find it anywhere else."
– Marvin Gaye

"Epochs of great confusion and general uncertainty in a given world contain the slumbering, not-yet-manifest seeds of clarity and certainty."
– Jean Gebser

"Of course, nothing that exists exists for its own sake; it exists for the sake of the whole."
— Jean Gebser

"Sometimes you will never know the value of a moment until it becomes a memory."
— Theodor Seuss Geisel

"You know you're in love when you don't want to fall asleep because reality is finally better than your dreams."
— Theodor Seuss Geisel

"Be who you are and say what you feel, because those who mind don't matter, and those who matter don't mind."
— Theodor Seuss Geisel

"By stretching yourself beyond your perceived level of confidence you accelerate your development of competence."
— Michael J. Gelb

"The river pulls you (yin) and pushes you (yang), but it is one river."
— Walter George

"Reason can answer questions, but imagination has to ask them."
— Ralph Gerard

"Self-confidence is the result of a successfully survived risk."
— Jack Gibb

"In short, we derive support for our preferred conclusions by listening to the words that we put in the mouths of people who have already been preselected for their willingness to say what we want to hear."
– Daniel Gilbert

"Forget not that the earth delights to feel your bare feet and the winds long to play with your hair."
– Khalil Gibran

"And forget not that the earth delights to feel your bare feet and the winds long to play with your hair."
– Kahlil Gibran

"Your pain is the breaking of the shell that encloses your understanding."
– Khalil Gibran

"Before you diagnose yourself with depression or low self-esteem, first make sure that you are not, in fact, just surrounded by assholes."
– William Gibson

"Believe those who are seeking the truth. Doubt those who find it."
– Andre Gide

"In order to be utterly happy the only thing necessary is to refrain from comparing this moment with other moments in the past – which I often did not fully enjoy because I was comparing them with other moments in the future."
– Andre Gide

"Those who find beauty in all of nature will find themselves at one with the secrets of life itself."
– L.W. Gilbert

"There are persons who seem to have overcome obstacles and by character and perseverance to have risen to the top. But we have no record of the numbers of able persons who fall by the wayside, persons who, with enough encouragement and opportunity, might make great contributions."
– Mary Barnett Gilson

"Follow your inner moonlight; don't hide the madness."
– Allen Ginsberg

"Success requires first expending ten units of effort to produce one unit of results. Your momentum will then produce ten units of results with each unit of effort."
– Charles J. Givens

"We learn by example and by direct experience because there are real limits to the adequacy of verbal instruction."
– Malcolm Gladwell

"Success isn't a result of spontaneous combustion. You must set yourself on fire."
– Arnold H. Glasgow

"For the first couple of years you make stuff, it's just not that good. It's trying to be good, it has potential, but it's not. A lot of people never get past this phase; they quit. We all go through this. And if you are just starting out or you are still in this phase, you gotta know it's normal and the most important thing you can do is do a lot of work. It is only by going through a volume of

work that you will close that gap, and your work will be as good as your ambitions."
– Ira Glass

"Are is a personal act of courage, something one human does that creates change in another."
– Seth Godin

"Trust in yourself, then you will know how to live."
– Johann Wolfgang von Goethe

"The struggle of the male to learn to listen to and respect his own intuitive, inner promptings is the greatest challenge of all. His conditioning has been so powerful that it has all but destroyed his ability to be self-aware."
– Herb Goldberg

"Trust in what you love, continue to do it, and it will take you where you need to go."
– Natalie Goldberg

"Who is the happiest of men? He who values the merits of others, and in their pleasure takes joy, even as though t'were his own."
– Johann Wolfgang von Goethe

"If you treat an individual as he is, he will remain how he is. But if you treat him as if he were what he ought to be and could be, he will become what he ought to be and could be."
– Johann Wolfgang von Goethe

"Thins that matter most must never be at the mercy of things that matter least."
– Johann Wolfgang von Goethe

"If you want a wise answer, ask a reasonable question."

– Johann Wolfgang Von Goethe

"The person born with a talent they are meant to use will find their greatest happiness in using it."

– Johann Wolfgang Von Goethe

"I have come to the frightening conclusion that I am the decisive element. It is my personal approach that creates the climate. It is my daily mood that makes the weather. I possess tremendous power to make life miserable or joyous. I can be a tool of torture or an instrument of inspiration, I can humiliate or humor, hurt or heal. In all situations, it is my response that decides whether a crisis is escalated or de-escalated, and a person is humanized or de-humanized. If we treat people as they are, we make them worse. If we treat people as they ought to be, we help them become what they are capable of becoming."

– Johann Wolfgang Von Goethe

"Treat people as if they were what they ought to be and you help them to become what they are capable of being."

– Johann Wolfgang Von Goethe

"Progress has not followed a straight ascending line, but a spiral with rhythms of progress and retrogression, of evolution and dissolution."

– Johann Wolfgang Von Goethe

"The heights charm us, but the steps do not; with the mountain in our view we love to walk the plains."

– Johann Wolfgang Von Goethe

"I have learned a great deal from illness that I never could have learned any other way."

– Johann Wolfgang von Goethe

"Treat people as if they were what they ought to be, and you can help them to become what they are capable of being."

– Johann Wolfgang von Goethe

"I have come to the frightening conclusion that I am the decisive element. It is my personal approach that creates the climate. It is my daily mood that makes the weather. I possess tremendous power to make life miserable or joyous. I can be a tool of torture or an instrument of inspiration, I can humiliate or humor, hurt or heal. In all situations, it is my response that decides whether a crisis is escalated or de-escalated, and a person is humanized or de-humanized. If we treat people as they are, we make them worse. If we treat people as they ought to be, we help them become what they are capable of becoming."

– Johann Wolfgang Von Goethe

"Doubt can only be removed by action."

– Johann Wolfgang von Goethe

"I have come to the frightening conclusion that I am the decisive element. It is my personal approach that creates the climate. It is my daily mood that makes the weather. I possess tremendous power to make life miserable or joyous. I can be a tool of torture or an instrument of inspiration, I can humiliate or humor, hurt or heal. In all situations, it is my response that decides whether a crisis is escalated or de-escalated, and a person is humanized or de-humanized. If we treat people as they are, we make them worse. If we treat people as they ought to be, we help them become what they are capable of becoming."

– Johann Wolfgang von Goethe

"There is no past that we can bring back by longing for it. There is only an eternally new now that builds and creates itself out of what is best as the past withdraws."

– Johann Wolfgang von Goethe

"The deed is everything, the glory nothing."

– Johann Wolfgang von Goethe

"Thousands of people who say they 'love' animals sit down once or twice a day to enjoy the flesh of creatures who have been utterly deprived of everything that could make their lives worth living and who endured the awful suffering and the terror of the abattoirs."

– Jane Goodall

"The best way I know to counteract despair is to do everything I can to make a difference, even in the smallest way, every day. To take some action to do something about at least some of the bad things that are going on as people work selflessly to make this a better world."

– Jane Goodall

"Journalism is the only profession explicitly protected by the U.S. Constitution, because journalists are supposed to be the check and balance on government. We're supposed to be holding those in power accountable. We're not supposed to be their megaphone. That's what the corporate media have become."

– Amy Goodman

"We're here for a reason. I believe a bit of the reason is to throw little torches out to lead people through the dark."

– Whoopi Goldberg

"Aspire to a certain gracefulness. Difficult to define, the French called it je ne sais quoi – it is a kind of sparkle, gallantry and zest; a wholeheartedness imbued with humor. It is carrying oneself with flair and pluck, a spontaneous ease and a light elegance."

– Baltasar Gracian

"Just or not, if you're openly skeptical about the truthfulness of others, it indicates that you yourself might be deceitful."

– Baltasar Gracian

"Be free to speak well of someone who speaks ill of you."

– Baltasar Gracian

"Anyone can stumble and fall, but a great person won't lie there and make it home."

– Baltasar Gracian

"The person most dangerous to you is yourself."

– Baltasar Gracian

"Learn how to take things. A knife taken by the blade will cut you, but taken by the handle it can be used as a tool."

– Baltasar Gracian

"I don't think about what I have done. I only think of the things I want to do, and I haven't done."

– Martha Graham

"There is a vitality, a life force, an energy, a quickening that is translated through you into action, and because there is only one of you in all time, this expression is unique. And if you block it, it will never exist through any other medium and will be lost."
– Martha Graham

"We must free ourselves of the hope that the sea will ever rest. We must learn to sail in high winds."
– Hanmer Parsons Grant

"Build your drams, or someone else will hire you to build theirs."
– Farrah Gray

"Men are motivated and empowered when they feel needed."
– John Gray

"Clearly no group can as an entity create ideas. Only individuals can do this. A group of individuals may, however, stimulate one another in the creation of ideas."
– Estill I. Green

"Understanding requires insight. Insight must be anchored."
– Brian Greene

"Life isn't about waiting for the storm to pass. It's about learning how to dance in the rain."
– Vivian Greene

"Work like you don't need the money, Love like your Heart has never been broken, and Dance like no one is watching!"
– Aurora Greenway

"Animals and humans suffer and die alike. Violence causes the same pain, the same spilling of blood, the same stench of death, the same arrogant, cruel and brutal taking of life. We don't have to be a part of it."
– Dick Gregory

"That's one of the great things about music. You can sing a song to 85,000 people and they'll sing it back for 85,000 different reasons."
– Dave Grohl

"The chief pang of most trials is not so much the actual suffering itself as our own spirit of resistance to it."
– Jean Nicolas Grou

"We all need friends with whom we can speak of our deepest concerns, and who do not fear to speak the truth in love to us."
– Margaret Guenther

"Sit on the train tracks and really believe a train won't come; lie in your house when it is inflamed and tell yourself that it really isn't burning; go ahead, neglect all sort of reason and continue to tell yourself that what you believe is the irrefutable truth and the day will come when you are wakened by a piercing whistle and scorching flames."
– Dave Guerrero

"True revolution is about tenderness."
– Che Guevara

"When you fail you learn from the mistakes you made and it motivates you to work ever harder."
– Natalie Gulbis

"There is nothing still. Life is never still. No plant, no animal no river. Can we think of Nature as a metaphor and keep ourselves constantly evolving?
– Anil Gupta

"Hard work doesn't guarantee success, but improves its chances."
– B.J. Gupta

# H

"Time is a factory where everyone slaves away earning enough love to break their own chains."
– Hafiz

"The great religions are the ships, poets the life boats. Every sane person I know has jumped overboard."
– Hafiz

"Love people who hate you. Pray for people who have wronged you. It won't just change their life, it will change yours."
– Mandy Hale

"A bad attitude can literally block love, blessings, and destiny from finding you. Don't be the reason you don't succeed."
– Mandy Hale

"I don't believe that consciousness is generated by the brain. I believe that the brain is more of a receiver of consciousness."
– Graham Hancock

"People will try to tell you that all of the great opportunities have been snapped up. In reality, the world changes every second, blowing new opportunities in all directions, including yours."
– Ken Hakuta

"I am only one, but I am one. I cannot do everything, but I can do something. And I will not let what I cannot do interfere with what I can do."
– Edward Everett Hale

"There is a very real relationship, both quantitatively and qualitatively, between what you contribute and what you get out of this world."
– Oscar Hammerstein II

"Mental time travel is one of the greatest gifts of the mind. It makes us human, and it makes us special."
– Claudia Hammond

"Sometimes your joy is the source of your smile, and sometimes your smile is the source of your joy."
– Thich Nhat Hanh

"Our own life is the instrument with which we experiment with the truth.
– Thich Nhat Hanh

"We are here to awaken from the illusion of our separateness."
– Thich Nhat Hanh

"Hope is important because it can make the present moment less difficult to bear. If we believe that tomorrow will be better, we can bear a hardship today."
– Thich Nhat Hanh

"We are here to awaken from the illusion of our separateness."
– Thich Nhat Hanh

"The only way you can truly control how you are seen is being honest all the time."
– Tom Hanks

"If it wasn't hard, everyone would do it. It's the hard that makes the great."
– Tom Hanks

"People inspire you, or they drain you – pick them wisely."
– Hans. F. Hansen

"I never let my subject get in the way of what I want to talk about."
– Mark Victor Hansen

"To will is to select a goal, determine a course of action that will bring one to that goal, and then hold to that action until the goal is reached. The key is action."
– Michael Hanson

"Every one of us receives and passes on an inheritance. The inheritance may not be an accumulation of earthly possessions or acquired riches, but whether we

realize it or not, our choices, words, actions, and values will impact someone and form the heritage we hand down.
– Ben Hardesty

"Thought is the wind and knowledge the sail."
– David Hare

"A billion people sitting watching their TV in the room that they call living. But as for me, I see living as loving. And since there is no loving room, I sit on the grass under a tree dreaming of the way things use to be, pre-industrial revolution."
– Woody Harrelson

"The moment you feel like you have to prove your worth to someone is the moment to absolutely and utterly walk away."
– Alysia Harris

"Consider it: every person you have ever met, every person will suffer the loss of his friends and family. All are going to lose everything they love in this world. Why would one want to be anything but kind to them in the meantime?"
– Sam Harris

"There's no point in burying a hatchet if you're going to put up a marker on the site."
– Sydney Harris

"The whole purpose of education is to turn mirrors into windows."
– Sydney Harris

"Many people feel 'guilty' about things they shouldn't feel guilty about, in order to shut out feelings of guilt about things they should feel guilty about."

– Sydney J. Harris

"Those who are lifting the world upward and onward are those who encourage more than criticize."

– Elizabeth Harrison

"Self-esteem is as important to our well-being as legs are to a table. It is essential for physical and mental health and for happiness."

– Louise Hart

"Self-esteem creates natural highs. Knowing that you're lovable helps you to love more. Knowing that you're important helps you to make a difference to others. Knowing that you are capable empowers you to create more. Knowing that you're valuable and that you have a special place in the universe is a serene spiritual joy in itself."

– Louise Hart

"The only sure thing about luck is that it will change."

– Bret Harte

"Wherever a man's consciousness is, there is the man himself, no matter whether his physical body is there or not."

– Franz Hartmann

"The exercise of power is determined by thousands of interactions between the world of the powerful and that of the powerless, all the more so because these worlds are never divided by a sharp line: everyone has a small part of himself in both."

— Vaclav Havel

"Hope is a state of mind, not of the world. Hope, in this deep and powerful sense, is not the same as joy that things are going well, or willingness to invest in enterprises that are obviously heading for success, but rather an ability to work for something because it is good."

— Vaclav Havel

"The end of the era of rationalism has been catastrophic. Armed with the same supermodern weapons, often from the same suppliers, and followed by television cameras, the members of various tribal cults are at war with one another.... The abyss between rational and the spiritual, the external and the internal, the objective and the subjective, the technical and the moral, the universal and the unique, constantly grows deeper."

— Vaclav Havel

"Ralph Waldo Emerson once asked what we would do if the stars only came out once every thousand years. No one would sleep that night, of course. The world would become religious overnight. We would be ecstatic, delirious, made rapturous by the glory of God. Instead the stars come out every night, and we watch television."

— Paul Hawkin

"A universal characteristic of genius is humility."

— David Hawkins

"Love is the great miracle cure. Loving ourselves works miracles in our lives."

– Louise Hay

"Can you forgive yourself for not being perfect? Can you release criticism and judgment of yourself and of other people?"

– Louise Hay

"Going over and over those past difficulties don't do anything but attract more difficulties to you."

– Louise Hay

"Be careful how you are talking to yourself, because you are listening."

– Lisa M. Hayes

"Gracefulness has been defined to be the outward expression of the inward harmony of the soul."

– William Hazlitt

"Never anticipate evils; or, because you cannot have things exactly as you wish, make them out worse than they are through spite and willfulness."

– William Hazlitt

"Wherever there is a human in need, there is an opportunity for kindness and to make a difference."

– Kevin Heath

"Four very powerful words to say to your child: I believe in you."

– Kevin Heath

"To him who looks upon the world rationally, the world in its turn presents a rational aspect. The relation is mutual."
– Georg Wilhelm Friedrich Hegel

"To dwell is to garden."
– Martin Heidegger

"To be a poet in a destitute time means: to attend, singing, to the trace of the fugitive gods. This is why the poet in the time of the world's night utters the holy."
– Martin Heidegger

"The possible ranks higher than the actual."
– Martin Heidegger

"Ability is a wonderful thing, but its value is greatly enhances by dependability. Ability implies repeatability and accountability."
– Robert A. Heinlein

"God help all children as they move into a time of life they don't understand and must struggle through the precepts picked from the garbage cans of older people, clinging to odds and ends that will mess them up for all time, or hating the trash so much they'll waste their future on the hatred."
– Lillian Hellman

"Now is no time to think of what you do not have. Think of what you can do with what there is."
– Ernest Hemingway

"Hesitation increases in relation to risk in equal proportion to age."
– Ernest Hemingway

"It is a good thing to have an end to journey toward; but it is the journey that matters, in the end."
– Ernest Hemingway

"Stop trying to perfect your child, but keep trying to perfect your relationship with him."
– Dr. Henker

"Are you bored with life? Then throw yourself into some work you believe in with all your heart, live for it, die for it, and you will find happiness that you had thought could never be yours."
– Audrey Hepburn

"I plant a garden to believe in tomorrow."
– Audrey Hepburn

"We are taught you must blame your father, your sisters, your brothers, the school, the teachers – but never blame yourself. It's never your fault. But it's always your fault, because if you wanted to change you're the one who has got to change."
– Katharine Hepburn

"Life is to be lived. If you have to support yourself, you had bloody well find some way that is going to be interesting. And you don't do that by sitting around."
– Katharine Hepburn

"Character is fate."
– Heraclitus

"Unless you expect the unexpected you will never find truth, for it is hard to discover and hard to attain."
– Heraclitus

"It is in changing that things find repose."
– Heraclitus

"The lord whose oracle is at Delphi neither speaks nor conceals, but gives signs."
– Heraclitus

"This universe, which is the same for all, has not been made by any god or man, but it always has been is, and will be - an ever-living fire, kindling itself by regular measures and going out by regular measures."
– Heraclitus

"You could not discover the limits of soul, even if you traveled by every path in order to do so; such is the depth of its meaning."
– Heraclitus

"The best of men choose one thing in preference to all else, immortal glory in preference to mortal good; whereas the masses simply glut themselves like cattle."
– Heraclitus

"Dare to be true: nothing can need a lie: A fault, which needs it most, grows thereby."
– George Herbert

"An open mind is like an open window. It lets the fresh air in."
– Mike Hernacki

"If having a soul means being able to feel love and loyalty and gratitude, then animals are better off than a lot of humans."
– James Herriot

"Happiness is a how, not a what; a talent, not an object."
– Hermann Hesse

"Chaos demands to be recognised and experienced before letting itself be converted into a new order."
– Herman Hesse

"The best things in life are never rationed. Friendship, loyalty, love, do not require coupons."
– George T. Hewitt

"I never got along with my dad. Kids used to come up to me and say, "My dad can beat up your dad." I'd say, "Yeah? When?"
– Bill Hicks

"Don't wait, the time will never be just right."
– Napoleon Hill

"Most great people have attained their greatest success one stop beyond their greatest failure."
– Napolean Hill

"The starting point of all achievement is desire. Keep this constantly in mind. Weak desire brings weak results, just as a small fire makes a small amount of heat."
– Napoleon Hill

"If you compromise with your own conscience, it will not be long before you will have no conscience because your conscience will fail to guide you, just as an alarm clock will fail to awaken you if you do not heed it."
– Napoleon Hill

"You don't have to be a fantastic hero to do certain things - to compete. You can be just an ordinary chap, sufficiently motivated to reach challenging goals."
– Sir Edmund Hillary

"If I am not for myself, who will be? And when I am for myself, what am 'I'? And if not now, when?"
– Hillel

"Set out each day believing in your dreams. Know without a doubt that you were made for amazing things."
– Josh Hinds

"Accept failure as a normal part of living. View it as part of the process of exploring your world; make a note of its lessons and move on."
– Tom Hobson

"It is easier to find a score of men wise enough to discover the truth than to find one intrepid enough, in the face of opposition, to stand up for it."
– A.A. Hodge

"It sometimes seems that intense desire creates not only its own opportunities, but its own talents."
– Eric Hoffer

"Fair play is primarily not blaming others for anything that is wrong with us."
– Eric Hoffer

"When people are free to do as they choose, they usually imitate each other."
– Eric Hoffer

"Life is a grindstone. Whether is grinds us down or polishes us up, depends on us."
– L. Thomas Holdcroft

"The past is a guidepost, not a hitching post."
– L. Thomas Holdcroft

"The miracle of gratitude is that it shifts your perception to such an extent that it changes the world you see."
– Robert Holden

"Don't flatter yourself that friendship authorizes you to say disagreeable things to your intimates. The nearer you come into relation with a person, the more necessary do tact and courtesy become."
– Oliver Wendell Holmes

"Any child who can spend an hour or two a day, or more if he wants, with adults that he likes who are interested in the world and like to talk about it, will on most days learn far more from their talk than he would learn in a week of school."
– John Holt

"Motivation is simple. You eliminate those who are not motivated."
– Lou Holtz

"It's not the load that breaks you down, it's the way you carry it."
– Lou Holtz

"Success is 99 percent failure."
– Soichiro Honda

"If you're faced with a forced landing, fly the thing as far into the crash as possible."

— Bob Hoover

"My philosophy is: It's none of my business what people say of me and think of me. I am what I am and I do what I do. I expect nothing and accept everything. And it makes life so much easier."

— Anthony Hopkins

"He who postpones the hour of living rightly is like the fool who waits for the river to run out before he crosses."

— Horace

"It's not the load that breaks you down, it's how you carry it."

— Lena Horne

"Tearing down the rest of the world won't make you happy. Look inside yourself. Because finding who you were meant to be? What you were put into this world to do? That's what fills the emptiness. It's the only thing that can."

— A.G. Howard

"Call it a clan, call it a network, call it a tribe, call it a family. Whatever you call it, whoever you are, you need one."

— Jane Howard

"Hold fast to dreams. For if dreams die, life is a broken-winged bird that cannot fly."

— James Langston Hughes

"There is one spectacle grander than the sea, that is the sky; there is one spectacle grander than the sky, that is the interior of the soul."
– Victor Hugo

"Not being heard is no reason for silence."
– Victor Hugo

"Where the telescope ends, the microscope begins. Which of the two has the grander view?"
– Victor Hugo

"To learn to read is to light a fire; every syllable that is spelled out is a spark."
– Victor Hugo

"Success is simple. First, you decide what you want specifically; and second, you decide you're willing to pay the price to make it happen, and then pay that price."
– Bunker Hunt

"Decide what you want, decide what you are willing to exchange for it. Establish your priorities and go to work."
– H.L. Hunt

"Goals are dreams with deadlines."
– Diana Scharf Hunt

"Love makes your soul crawl out from its hiding place."
– Zora Neale Hurst

"There's only one corner of the universe you can be certain of improving, and that's your own self."
– Aldous Huxley

"Facts do not cease to exist because they are ignored."
– Aldous Huxley

"The secret of genius is to carry the spirit of the child into old age, which means never losing your enthusiasm."
– Aldous Huxley

"Vision is not won by making an effort to get it: it comes to those who have learned to put their minds and eyes into a state of alert passivity, of dynamic relaxation."
– Aldous Huxley

"After silence, that which comes nearest to expressing the inexpressible is music."
– Aldous Huxley

"The meat industry spends hundreds of millions of dollars lying to the public about their product. But no amount of false propaganda can sanitize meat. The facts are absolutely clear: Eating meat is bad for human health, catastrophic for the environment, and a living nightmare for animals."
– Chrissie Hynde

# I

"In times of great stress or adversity, it's always best to keep busy, to plow your anger and your energy into something positive."
– Lee Iacocca

"Leave behind the passive dreaming of a rose-tinted future. The energy of happiness exists in living today with roots sunk firmly in reality's soil."
– Daisaku Ikeda

"We have enslaved the rest of animal creation and have treated our distant cousins in fur and feathers so badly that beyond doubt, if they were to formulate a religion, they would depict the Devil in human form."
– William Ralph Inge

"You will rise by lifting others."
– Robert G. Ingersoll

"Half my life is an act of revision."
– John Irving

"Little minds are tamed and subdued by misfortune; but great minds rise above them."
– Washington Irving

"Don't be afraid to be amazing."
– Andy Offutt Irwin

"You shouldn't get disillusioned when you get knocked back. All you've discovered is that the search is difficult, and you still have a duty to keep on searching."
– Kazuo Ishiguro

# J

"Set your goals high, and don't stop until you get there."
— Bo Jackson

"I wasn't exactly brought up in one of those Norman Rockwell paintings you used to see on the cover of the *Saturday Evening Post*."
— Reggie Jackson

"If you can't figure out your purpose, figure out your passion. For your passion will lead you right into your purpose."
— T.D. Jakes

"To take what there is and use it, without waiting forever in vain for the preconceived – to dig deep into the actual and get something out of that – this doubtless is the right way to live."
– Henry James

"The accumulation of small, optimistic acts produces quality in our culture and in your life. Our culture resonates in tense times to individual acts of grace."
– Jennifer James

"Act as if what you do makes a difference. It does."
– William James

"The art of being wise is knowing what to overlook."
– William James

"Life can not give me joy and peace, it is up to me to will it. Life just gives me time and space, it is up to me to fill it."
– William James

"Whenever you're in conflict with someone, there is one factor that can make the difference between damaging your relationship and deepening it. That factor is attitude."
– William James

"The devil's happy when the critics run you off."
– Criss Jami

"If we are going to do anything significant with life, we sometimes have to move away from it – beyond the usual measurements. We must occasionally follow visions and dreams."
– Bede Jarrett

"We're still not where we're going, but we're still not where we were."
— Natasha Jasefowitz

"Determine never to be idle. No person will have occasion to complain of the want of time who never loses any. It is wonderful how much may be done if we are always doing."
— Thomas Jefferson

"Never be haughty to the humble, never be humble to the haughty."
— Thomas Jefferson

"One life is all we have and we live it as we believe in living it. But to sacrifice what you are and to live without belief, that is a fate more terrible than dying."
— Joan of Arc

"Here's to the crazy ones, the misfits, the rebels, the troublemakers, the round pegs in the square holes...the ones who see things differently – they're not fond of rules. You can quote them, disagree with them, glorify or vilify them, but the only thing you can't do is ignore them because they change things... they push the human race forward, and while some may see them as the crazy ones, we see genius, because the ones who are crazy enough to think that they can change the world, are the ones who do."
— Steve Jobs

"I think music in itself is healing. It's an explosive expression of humanity. It's something we are all touched by. No matter what culture we're from, everyone loves music."
— Billy Joel

"You are not likely to get anywhere in particular if you don't know where you want to go."
– Percy H. Johnson

"If a man does not make new acquaintance as he advances through life, he will soon find himself left alone. A man, Sir, should keep his friendship in constant repair."
– Dr. Samuel Johnson

"When it comes to living your purpose, every day is the day, every time is the time, and everywhere is the place."
– Harley "Durianrider" Johnstone

"To avoid critics: Don't do anything, don't say anything, don't stand for anything, don't be anything."
– Harley "Durianrider" Johnstone

"Be careful of your actions. You never know when you're creating a memory."
– Ricki Lee Jones

"Only the boring are bored."
– Tommy Lee Jones

"And the trouble is, if you don't risk anything, you risk even more."
– Erica Jong

"You must expect great things of yourself before you can do them."
– Michael Jordan

"If you're trying to achieve, there will be roadblocks. I've had them; everybody has had them. But obstacles don't have to stop you. If you run into a wall, don't turn around and give up. Figure out how to climb it, go through it, or work around it."

– Michael Jordan

"One who has imagination without learning has wings without feet."

– Joseph Joubert

"I have come to accept the feeling of not knowing where I am going. And I have trained myself to love it. Because it is only when we are suspended in mid-air with no landing in sight, that we force our wings to unravel and alas begin our flight. And as we fly, we still may not know where we are going to. But the miracle is in the unfolding of the wings. You may not know where you're going, but you know that so long as you spread your wings, the winds will carry you."

– C. JoyBell

"The future of mankind very much depends upon the recognition of the shadow."

– Carl Gustav Jung

"Nothing has a stronger influence psychologically on their environment, and especially on their children, than the unlived life of the parents."

– Carl Gustav Jung

"Even a happy life cannot be without a measure of darkness, and the word 'happy' would lose its meaning if it were not balanced by sadness. It is far better to take things as they come along with patience and equanimity."

– Carl Gustav Jung

"The shoe that fits one person pinches another; there is no recipe for living that suits all cases."
– Carl Gustav Jung

"One does not become enlightened by imagining figures of light, but by making the darkness conscious."
– Carl Gustav Jung

"An understanding heart is everything in a teacher, and cannot be esteemed highly enough. One looks back with appreciation to the brilliant teachers, but with gratitude to those who touched our human feelings. The curriculum is so much necessary raw material, but warmth is the vital element for the growing plant and for the soul of the child."
– Carl Gustav Jung

"I simply believe that some part of the human Self or Soul is not subject to the laws of space and time."
– Carl Gustav Jung

"The only important thing is to follow nature. A tiger should be a good tiger; a tree, a good tree. So man should be a man. But to know what man is, one must follow Nature and go on alone, admitting the importance of the unexpected. Still, nothing is possible without love – for love puts one in a mood to risk everything, and not to withhold important elements."
– Carl Gustav Jung

"We still attribute to the other fellow all the evil and inferior qualities that we do not like to recognize in ourselves, and therefore have to criticize and attack him, when all that has happened is that an inferior "soul" has emigrated from one person to another. The world is still full of betes noires and scapegoats, just as it formerly teemed with witches and werewolves."

– Carl Gustav Jung

"In all chaos there is cosmos, in all disorder a secret order."

– Carl Gustav Jung

"Your vision will become clear only when you look into your heart. Who looks outside, dreams. Who looks inside awakens."

– Carl Gustav Jung

# K

"Some people try to tell you the things you want in life are out of your grasp, while others lift you up on their shoulders and help you reach them. I may not know a lot, but I prefer to fill my life with people who let me climb on top of their shoulders, not people who try to keep me planted on the ground."
– Katie Kacvinsky

"An innovation is one of those things that society looks at and says, 'If we make this part of the way we live and work, it will change the way we live and work.'"
– Dean Kamen

"Find a seed at the bottom of your heart and bring forth a flower."
– Shigenori Kameoka

"If man is not to stifle his human feelings, he must practice kindness towards animals. For he who is cruel to animals becomes hard also in his dealings with men. We can judge the heart of a man by his treatment of animals."
– Immanuel Kant

"Some people grumble because roses have thorns; I am thankful that the thorns have roses."
– Jean-Baptiste Alphonse Karr

"You can't always be happy, but you can almost always be profoundly aware and curious, and reap the psychological and physical benefits. Thankfully, curiosity is not a fixed characteristic. It's a strength we can develop and wield on the path to a more fulfilling life."
– Todd Kashdan

"The economy depends about as much on economists as the weather does on weather forecasters."
– Jean-Paul Kauffmann

"The best way to predict the future is to invent it."
– Alan Kay

"The real meaning of enlightenment is to gaze with undimmed eyes on all darkness."
– Nikos Kazantzakis

"Do you not see how necessary a world of pains and troubles is to school an intelligence and make it a soul?"
– John Keats

"The lines of giving are complicated, you never know how it will come back. But you have to give because you can't let the cord break with you."
– Maria Diarra Keita

"My father didn't tell me how to live; he lived, and let me watch him do it."
– Clarence Budington Kelland

"Defeat is simply a signal to press onward."
– Helen Keller

"I am only one; but still I am one. I cannot do everything, but still I can do something; I will not refuse to do something I can do."
– Helen Keller

"We could never learn to be brave and patient, if there were only joy in the world."
– Helen Keller

"Many persons have a wrong idea of what constitutes true happiness. It is not attained through self-gratification, but through fidelity to a worthy purpose."
– Helen Keller

"And children whose backgrounds have stunted their sense of the future need to be taught by example that they are good for more than they dared dream."
– Kenneth Keniston

"Nothing compares to the simple pleasure of a bike ride."
– John F. Kennedy

"It is better to be boldly decisive and risk being wrong than to agonize at length and be right too late."
– Marilyn Moats Kennedy

"Is not this, perhaps, the secret of every true and great mystery, that it is simple? Does it not love secrecy for that very reason? Proclaimed, it were but a word;

kept silent it is being. And a miracle too, in the sense that being with all its paradoxes is miraculous."
– C. Kerenyi

"The only people for me are the mad ones, the ones who are mad to live, mad to talk, mad to be saved, desirous of everything at the same time, the ones who never yawn or say a commonplace thing, but burn, burn, burn, like fabulously yellow roman candles exploding like spiders across the stars."
– Jack Kerouac

"The only people for me are the mad ones, the ones who are mad to live, mad to talk, mad to be saves, desirous of everything at the same time, the ones who never yawn or say a common place thing, but burn, burn, bur, like fabulous yellow roman candles exploding like spiders across the stars and in the middle you see the blue centerlight pop and everybody goes, 'Awww!'"
– Jack Kerouac

"Believe in the holy contour of life."
– Jack Kerouac

"Of all the things I have learned in my lifetime, the one with the greatest value is that unexpected kindness is the most powerful, least costly and most underrated agent of human change."
– Bob Kerrey

"Keep thy airspeed up, less the earth come from below and smite thee."
– William Kershner

"There will always be a frontier where there is an open mind and a willing hand."
– Charles F. Kettering

"A loving person lives in a loving world. A hostile person lives in a hostile world. Everyone you meet is your mirror."
– Ken Keys

"Everything in life is speaking in spite of its apparent silence."
– Hazrat Inayat Khan

"Listen with an open heart and an open mind to those who love you the most. You may hear a grain of truth that will later become the foundations of your entire belief system."
– Callie Khouri

"Face the facts of being what you are, for that is what changes what you are."
– Søren Kierkegaard

"Life can only be understood backwards, but it has to be lived forwards."
– Søren Kierkegaard

"There comes a time when one must take a position that is neither safe, nor politic, nor popular, but he must take it because conscience tells him it is right."
– Martin Luther King, Jr.

"Take the first step in faith. You don't have to see the whole staircase. Just take the first step."
– Marin Luther King, Jr.

"Never, never be afraid to do what's right, especially if the well-being of a person or animal is at stake. Society's punishments are small compared to the wounds we inflict on our soul when we look the other way."

– Martin Luther King, Jr.

"Forgiveness is not an occasional act – it is an attitude."

– Martin Luther King, Jr.

"We must develop and maintain the capacity to forgive. He who is devoid of the power to forgive is devoid of the power to love. There is some good in the worst of us and some evil in the best of us."

– Martin Luther King, Jr.

"All of life is interrelated. We are all caught in an inescapable network of mutuality, tied to a single garment of destiny. Whatever affects one directly affects all indirectly."

– Martin Luther King Jr.

"Our lives begin to end the day we become silent about things that matter."

– Martin Luther King, Jr.

"We must accept finite disappointment, but never lose infinite help."

– Martin Luther King, Jr.

"You don't have to have a college degree to serve. You don't have to make your subject and verb agree to serve. You only need a heart full of grace. A soul generated by love."

– Martin Luther King, Jr.

"Let no man pull you low enough to hate him."
– Martin Luther King, Jr.

"Philanthropy is commendable, but it must not cause the philanthropist to overlook the circumstances of economic injustice which make philanthropy necessary."
– Martin Luther King, Jr.

"Be like the single blade of grass. For she too, has been trampled on, mowed down, and hit with such bitterly cold stretches that she had to shut down to survive. Yet still she stands upright with dignity, knowing that she endures, and still she dances with the wind."
– Sandra King

"As your mind and body grow accustomed to a certain amount of sleep each night, so can you train your waking mind to sleep creatively and work out the vividly imagined waking dreams which are successful works of fiction."
– Stephen King

"Books are a uniquely portable magic."
– Stephen King

"You have powers you never dreamed of. You can do things you never thought you could do."
– Darwin Kingsley

"Growing food was the first activity that gave us enough prosperity to stay in one place, form complex social groups, tell our stories, and build our cities."
– Barbara Kingsolver

"The game is so large that one sees but a little at a time."
– Rudyard Kipling

"The words 'I am...' are important words; be careful what you hitch them to. The think you're claiming has a way of reaching back and claiming you."
– A.L. Kitselman

"As you put into practice the qualities of patience, punctuality, sincerity, and solicitude, you will have a better opinion of the world around you."
– Grenville Kleiser

"The will to win is not nearly so important as the will to prepare to win."
– Bobby Knight

"Creativity, as has been said, consists largely of rearranging what we know in order to find out what we do not know. Hence, to think creatively, we must be able to look afresh at what we normally take for granted."
– George Kneller

"I discovered I always have choices and sometimes it's only a choice of attitude."
– Judith M. Knowlton

"You don't ever have to feel guilty about removing toxic people from your life. It doesn't matter whether someone is a relative, romantic interest, employer, childhood friend, or a new acquaintance. You don't' have to make room for people who cause you pain or make you feel small. It's one thing if a person owns up to their behavior and makes an effort to change. But, if a person disregards your feelings, ignores your boundaries, and continues to treat you in a harmful way, they need to go."
– Danielle Koepke

"Often the search proves more profitable than the goal."
– E. L. Konigsburg

"The functions of intellect are insufficient without courage, love, friendship, compassion, and empathy."
– Dean Koontz

"To succeed, we must first believe that we can."
– Michael Korda

"Forgiveness is not just about the other. It's really for the beauty of your soul. It's for your own capacity to fulfill your life."
– Jack Kornfield

"The door to the next frontier is through your heart."
– Giselle Koy

"We are raised on comparison; our education is based on it, so is our culture. So we struggle to be someone other than who we are."
– Jiddu Krishnamurti

"The highest form of intelligence is the ability to observe without evaluating."
– Jiddu Krishnamurti

"We carry about us the burden of what thousands of people have said and the memories of all our misfortunes. To abandon all that is to be alone, and the mind that is alone is not only innocent but young – not in time or age, but young, innocent, alive at whatever age – and only such a mind can see that which is truth and that which is not measurable by words."
– Jiddu Krishnamurti

"The most beautiful people we have known are those who have known defeat, known suffering, known struggle, known loss, and have found their way out of the depths. These persons have an appreciation, a sensitivity, and an understanding of life that fills them with compassion, gentleness, and a deep loving concern. Beautiful people do not just happen."
– Elisabeth Kubler-Ross

"It's only when we truly know and understand that we have a limited time on earth – and that we have no way of knowing when our time is up, we will then begin to live each day to the fullest, as if it was the only one we had."
– Elizabeth Kubler-Ross

"People are like stained-glass windows. They sparkle and shine when the sun is out, but when the darkness sets in their true beauty is revealed only if there is light from within."
– Elisabeth Kubler-Ross

"The sun is by no means an old star, and its planets are mere children in cosmic age, so it seems likely that there are billions of planets in the universe not only where intelligent life is on a lower scale than man but other billions where it is approximately equal and others still where it is hundreds of thousands of millions of years in advance of us. When you think of the giant technological strides that man has made in a few millenia – less than a microsecond in the chronology of the universe – can you imagine the evolutionary development that much older life forms have taken? They may have progressed from biological species, which are fragile shells for the mind at best, into immortal machine entities – and then, over innumerable eons, they could emerge from the chrysalis of matter transformed into beings of pure energy and spirit. Their potentialities would be limitless and their intelligence ungraspable by humans."

– Stanley Kubrick

"The age of the alibi, in which we find ourselves, began with the opening sentence of Rousseau's Emile: 'Nature made me happy and good, and if I am otherwise, it is society's fault.'"

– Stanley Kubrick

"When I look at the kids training today, I can tell which ones are going to do well. It's not necessarily the ones who have the most natural talent or who fall the least. Sometimes it's the kids who fall the most, and keep pulling themselves up and trying again."

– Michelle Kwan

# L

"Man is so made that when anything fires his soul, impossibilities vanish."
– Jean de La Fontaine

"If one can actually revert to the truth, then a great deal of one's suffering can be erased – because a great deal of one's suffering is based on sheer lies."
– R.D. Laing

"Consider the following. We humans are social beings. We come into the world as the result of others' actions. We survive here in dependence on others. Whether we like it or not, there is hardly a moment of our lives when we do not benefit from others' activities. For this reason it is hardly surprising that most of our

happiness arises in the context of our relationships with others."
– Dalai Lama (Tenzin Gyatso)

"The true essence of humankind is kindness. There are other qualities which come from education or knowledge, but it is essential, if one wishes to be a genuine human being and impart satisfying meaning to one's existence, to have a good heart."
– Dalai Lama (Tenzin Gyatso)

"Hard times build determination and inner strength. Through them we can also come to appreciate the uselessness of anger. Instead of getting angry nurture a deep caring and respect for troublemakers because by creating such trying circumstances they provide us with invaluable opportunities to practice tolerance and patience."
– Dalai Lama (Tenzin Gyatso)

"Love and compassion are necessities, not luxuries. Without them, humanity cannot survive."
– Dalai Lama (Tenzin Gyatso)

"Violence is like a very strong pill. For a certain illness, it may be very useful, but the side effects are enormous. On a practical level it's very complicated, so it's much safer to avoid acts of violence."
– Dalai Lama (Tenzin Gyatso)

"Thousands, millions and billions of animals are killed for food. That is very sad. We human beings can live without meat, especially in our modern world. We have a great variety of vegetables and other supplementary foods, so we have the capacity and the responsibility to save billions of lives. I have seen many

individuals and groups promoting animal rights and following a vegetarian diet. This is excellent."
– Dalai Lama (Tenzin Gyatso)

"Change in the world comes from individuals, from the inner peace in individual hearts. Just as ripples spread out when a single pebble is dropped into water, the actions of individuals can have far-reaching effects."
– Dalai Lama (Tenzin Gyatso)

"There will come a time when you believe everything is finished. That will be the beginning."
– Louis L'Amour

"Some say opportunity knocks only once. That is not true. Opportunity knocks all the time, but you have to be ready for it. If the chance comes, you must have the equipment to take advantage of it."
– Louis L'Amour

"Hope begins in the dark, the stubborn hope that if you just show up and try to do the right thing, the dawn will come. You wait and watch and work: you don't give up."
– Anne Lamott

"It is not what you do for your children, but what you have taught them to do for themselves that will make them successful human beings."
– Ann Landers

"We talk on principal, but act on motivation."
– Walter Savage Landor

"Mix ignorance with arrogance at low altitude and the results are almost guaranteed to be spectacular."
– Bruce Landsberg

"Of all the things you wear, your expression is the most important."
— Janet Lane

"Flying is done largely with the imagination."
— Wolfgang Langewiesche

"The future turns out to be something that you make instead of find. It isn't waiting for your arrival, either with an arrest warrant or a band, nor is it any further away than the next sentence, the next best guess, the next sketch for the painting of a life portrait that might become a masterpiece. The future is an empty canvas or a blank sheet of paper, and if you have the courage of your own thought and your own observation, you can make it what you will."
— Lewis Lapham

"Every aspect of our lives is, in a sense, a vote for the kind of world we want to live in."
— Frances Moore Lappe

"Like a plant that starts up in showers and sunshine and does not know which has best helped it to grow, it is difficult to say whether the hard things or the pleasant things did me the most good."
— Lucy Larcom

"There's only us, there's only this. Forget regret, or life is yours to miss. No other road, no other way, no day but today."
— Jonathan Larson

"I understand that the most important encounter in life is the encounter with oneself."
— Yves Saint Laurent

"Nothing so much prevents our being natural as the desire of appearing so."
– D.H. Lawrence

"All men dream, but not equally. Those who dream by night in the dusty recesses of their minds, wake in the day to find that it was vanity: but the dreamers of the day are dangerous men, for they may act on their dreams with open eyes, to make them possible."
– T.E. Lawrence

"Most of the time we think the world is known and understood but this is a mistake. It is as if we live in a corridor and do not realise that a whole world lies beyond. It is by finding the cracks in the corridor of our current thoughts that we are able to catch sight of the world as a whole."
– Hilary Lawson

"I place a high moral value on the way people behave. I find it repellent to have a lot, and to behave with anything other than courtesy in the old sense of the word – politeness of the heart, a gentleness of the spirit."
– Fran Lebowitz

"We're destroying the Earth at a rate comparable with the impact of a giant asteroid slamming into the planet, or even a shower of vast heavenly bodies."
– Dr. Richard Leakey

"The key to immortality is first living a life worth remembering."
– Bruce Lee

"I fear not the man who has practiced 10,000 kickes, but I do fear the man who has practiced one kick 10,000 times."

– Bruce Lee

"Those who are unaware they are walking in darkness will never see the light."

– Bruce Lee

"Surround yourself with the dreamers and the doers, the believers and the thinkers. But most of all, surround yourself with those who see the greatness within you, even when you don't see it in yourself."

– Edmund Lee

"Be mindful of your self-talk. It's a conversation with the universe."

– David James Lees

"It is curious that with the advent of the automobile and the airplane, the bicycle is still with us. Perhaps people like the world they can see from a bike, or the air they breathe when they're out on a bike. Or they like the bicycle's simplicity and the precision with which it is made. Or because they like the feeling of being able to hurtle through air one minute, and saunter through a park the next, without leaving behind clouds of choking exhaust, without leaving behind so much as a footstep."

– Gurdon S. Leete

"It is good to have an end to journey toward; but it is the journey that matters, in the end."

– Ursula K. Le Guin

"I think our society is run by insane people for insane objectives. I think we're being run by maniacs for maniacal ends. I think they're all insane. But I am liable to be put away as insane for expressing that. That's what is insane about it."

– John Lennon

"When it gets down to having to use violence, then you are playing the system's game. The establishment will irritate you: pull your beard, flick your face to make you fight. Because once they've got you violent, then they know how to handle you. The only thing they don't know how to handle is non-violence and humor."

– John Lennon

"Real change starts with changing the game."

– Annie Leonard

"It seems to me that my whole life I've been standing on some tower or a pillbox or a trampoline, waving the names of writers, as if we needed rescue. And the first person I had to rescue was myself."

– John Leonard

"Personality can open doors, but only character can keep them open."

– Elmer G. Letterman

"Don't watch the clock: do what it does. Keep going.

– Sam Levenson

"The relationship with the other puts me into question, empties of myself and empties me without end, showing me ever new resources. I didn't know I was so rich, but I no longer have the right to keep anything for myself."

– Emmanuel Levinas

"The most important lessons in life can never be expressed in black and white, but must be experienced. Experience is the greatest teacher."
— Benny Lewis

"We read to know we are not alone."
— C. S. Lewis

"For what you see and hear depends a good deal on where you are standing: it also depends on what sort of person you are."
— C.S. Lewis

"Love is something more stern and splendid than mere kindness."
— C.S. Lewis

"Humans are amphibians - half spirit and half animal. As spirits they belong to the eternal world, but as animals they inhabit time."
— CS Lewis

"You are never too old to set another goal or to dream a new dream."
— C.S. Lewis

"To love at all is to be vulnerable."
— C.S. Lewis

"The best way to predict the future is to create it."
— Abraham Lincoln

"Have I not destroyed the enemy when I have made him into my friend?"
— Abraham Lincoln

"I do not destroy my enemies when I make them my friends."
— Abraham Lincoln

"If you surrender completely to the moments as they pass, you live more richly those moments."
— Anne Morrow Lindbergh

"Living in dreams of yesterday we find ourselves still dreaming of impossible future conquests."
— Charles Lindbergh

"I don't believe in taking foolish chances, but nothing can be accomplished without taking any chances at all."
— Charles A. Lindbergh

"While one person hesitates because he feels inferior, the other is busy making mistakes and becoming superior."
— Henry Link

"If we can transform ourselves, we have the potential to change the world."
— Laura van Dernoot Lipsky

"The eruption of feelings & emotions that follows a near-death experience, or any event that causes us to stop & look deeply at the reality of our lives, is ripe with the potential for insight & clarity."
— Allan Lokos

"Coaches who can outline plays on a black board are a dime a dozen. The ones who win get inside their player and motivate."
— Vince Lombardi

"You can't wait for inspiration. You have to go after it with a club."
– Jack London

"Age is opportunity no less than youth itself, though in another dress, and as the evening twilight fades away the sky is filled with stars, invisible by day."
– Henry Wadsworth Longfellow

"Most people would succeed in small things if they were not troubled with great ambitions."
– Henry Wadsworth Longfellow

"We judge ourselves by what we feel capable of doing, while others judge use by what we have already done."
– Henry Wadsworth Longfellow

"It is a sign of strength, not of weakness, to admit that you don't know all the answers."
– John P. Longhrane

"When I dare to be powerful – to use my strength in the service of my vision, then it becomes less and less important whether I am afraid."
– Audre Lorde

"After all these years, I am still involved in the process of self-discovery. It's better to explore life and make mistakes than to play it safe. Mistakes are part of the dues one pays for a full life."
– Sophia Loren

"Beauty is how you feel inside, and it reflects in your eyes. It is not something physical."
– Sophia Loren

"It's good to have money and the things that money can buy, but it's good, too, to make sure that you haven't lost the things that money can't buy."
— George Horace Lorimer

"The foolish and the dead never change their opinions."
— James Russell Lowell

"Rest is not idleness, and to lie sometimes on the grass under trees on a summer's day, listening to the murmur of the water, or watching the clouds float across the sky, is by no means a waste of time."
— John Lubbock

"Forgiveness is unlocking the door to set someone free, and realizing you were the prisoner."
— Max Lucado

"Always remember, your focus determines your reality."
— George Lucas

"The world's people all share the earnest aspiration to have peace, stability, justice, and cooperation."
— Tran Duc Luong

"Although we are in different boats, you in your boat and we in our canoe, we share the same river of life."
— Chief Oren Lyons

"What about the seventh generation? Where are you taking them? What will they have?"
— Chief Oren Lyons

# M

"In the course of history, there comes a time when humanity is called to shift to a new level of consciousness, to reach a higher moral ground. A time when we have to shed our fear and give hope to each other. That time is now."
– Wangari Maathai

"The question for each man to settle is not what he would do if he had means, time, influence, and educational advantages, but what he will do with the things he has."
– Hamilton Wright Mabie

"There's no security on this earth, only opportunity."
– Douglas MacArthur

"The world is in a constant conspiracy against the brave. It's the age-old struggle, the roar of the crowd on one side, the voice of your conscience on the other."
– Douglas MacArthur

"Travelers, there is no path, paths are made by walking."
– Antonio Machado

"It is much more secure to be feared than to be loved."
– Niccolo Machiavelli

"Never give advice unless you have walked the walk, because anybody can talk the talk."
– Valencia Mackie

"The church says the earth is flat, but I know that it is round, for I have seen the shadow on the moon, and I have more faith in a shadow than in the church."
– Ferdinand Magellan

"You are the one who can stretch your own horizon."
– Edgar F. Magnin

"Often the difference between a successful person and a failure is not one's better abilities or ideas, but the courage that one has to bet on one's ideas, to take a calculated risk – and to act."
– Andre Malraux

"Life is funny. Things change, people change, but you will always be you, so stay true to yourself and never sacrifice who you are for anyone."
– Zayn Malik

"We must have the courage to bet on our ideas, to take the calculated risk, and to act. Everyday living requires courage if life is to be effective and bring happiness."
– Maxwell Maltz

"Man's goodness is the flame that can never be extinguished."
– Nelson Mandela

"There is no passion to be found in settling for a life that is less than the one you are capable of living."
– Nelson Mandela

"The greatest glory in living lies not in never failing, but in rising every time we fail."
– Nelson Mandela

"There is no passion to be found playing small – in settling for a life that is less than the one you are capable of living."
– Nelson Mandela

"Beginning today, treat everyone you meet as if they were going to be dead by midnight."
– Og Mandino

"Hold every moment sacred. Give each clarity and meaning, each the weight of thine awareness, each its true and due fulfillment."
– Thomas Mann

"People will always have opinions about your decision because they're not courageous enough to take action on their opinion."
– Steve Maraboli

"When I accept myself, I am freed from the burden of needing you to accept me."
– Steve Maroboli

"As I look back on my life, I realize that every time I thought I was being rejected from something good, I was actually being re-directed to something better."
– Steve Maraboli

"A kind gesture can reach a wound that only compassion can heal."
– Steve Maraboli

"There is a wonderful mythical law of nature that the three things we crave most in life – happiness, freedom, and peace of mind – are always attained by giving them to someone else."
– Peyton Conway March

"A will finds a way."
– Orison Swett Marden

"Most obstacles melt away when we make up our minds to walk boldly through them."
– Orison Swett Marden

"You must bring every particle of your energy, unanswerable resolution, your best efforts, your persistent industry to your task or the best will not come out of you. You must back up your ambition by your whole nature, by unbounded enthusiasm and a determination to win which knows no failure."
– Orison Swett Marden

"I will not die an unlived life. I will not live in fear of falling or catching fire. I choose to inhabit my days, to allow my living to open me, to make me less afraid, more accessible, to loosen my heart until it becomes a wing, a torch, a promise. I choose to risk my significance; to live so that which came to me as a seed goes to the next as a blossom and that which came to me as a blossom, goes on as fruit."

– Dawna Markova

"When you think about our planet, it is one huge living body because of the water that flows through it. And, across the land masses you can have veins of water and arteries of water flowing. This flows into our ocean, which is the heart of our earth, and it exhales, evaporates water and puts water back into the hydrologic cycle, which then again goes up to the mountain tops and then again they form veins and arteries. So, our planet is just one, huge living body with water constantly circulating through it, and it is the water that gives it life. We too are like the surface of our planet, 70% water and 30% solid. We too have a heart. We have 60 thousand miles of veins and arteries. And just like the earth recycles the water, we have a water cycle within us."

– William E. Marks

"There is great hunger and thirst in all of us for the truth whether we are aware of it or not. There is no-one unfeeling or unseeing. To think ourselves unique is the height of ignorance."

– Agnes Martin

"The greatness of a man is not in how much wealth he acquires, but in his integrity and his ability to affect those around him positively."

– Bob Marley

"There is nothing we like to see so much as the gleam of pleasure in a person's eye when he feels that we have sympathized with him, understood him. At these moments something find and spiritual passes between two friends. These are the moments worth living."
– Don Marquis

"Good timber does not grow with ease. The stronger the wind the stronger the trees."
– J. Willard Marriott

"Let us be content to wait and see what will happen, but give us the determination to make the right things happen."
– Peter Marshall

"When we long for life without difficulties, remind us that oaks grow strong in contrary winds and diamonds are made under pressure."
– Peter Marshall

"Small deeds done are better than great deeds planned."
– Peter Marshall

"Besides the practical knowledge which defeat offers, there are important personality profits to be taken. Defeat strips away false values and makes you realize what you really want."
– William M. Marston

"The young man and woman with sight sees things as they are. The young man and woman with insight, sees things as they could be."
– Joseph P. Martino

"The philosophers have only interpreted the world, in various ways. The point, however, is to change it."
– Karl Marx

"Art is always and everywhere the secret confession, and at the same time the immortal movement of its time."
– Karl Marx

"To the man who only has a hammer in the toolkit, every problem looks like a nail."
– Abraham Maslow

"You were born an original. Don't die a copy."
– John Mason

"Like all weak men he laid an exaggerated stress on not changing one's mind."
– W. Somerset Maugham

"Simplicity and naturalness are the truest marks of distinction."
– W. Somerset Maugham

"Every worthwhile accomplishment has a price tag attached to it. The question is always whether you are willing to pay the price to attain it – in hard work, sacrifice, patience, faith, and endurance."
– John C. Maxwell

"People often say that those who are successful are lucky. As if it was by luck that they worked so hard to get successful. It wasn't luck, it was work. While the successful ones were practicing and working to create such luck, others who think the successful ones are lucky were out getting drunk, or staring at the TV, or being slothful, or shopping, or not doing what would have brought them such 'luck.'

If you want things in your life to happen, you have to work and make them happen. Nobody will do it for you. Certainly, 'luck' will not."

– John McCabe

"Oh, jealous lover, why so paranoid and concerned? If you took your lover to a bellydancing restaurant, would you also get jealous there, just because of the looking and the watching? Or would you cover your lover's eyes with couscous? Why not appreciate the site of beauty, and let others do the same? Maybe it is you who isn't the trusted one."

– John McCabe

"Many people spend so much time staring at the TV that is has become some sort of their reality. But it is a fake reality. It is similar to getting lost in some sort of surreal video game. But instead of them playing it, they are being played. They are the game pieces of the electronic mechanism guiding them in what to think, eat, wear, say, do, and purchase, and how to spend time, where to go, how to get there, who to go with, and what to say, enjoy, and listen to. It is a degradation of the human spirit, a tarnisher of the soul. It is the dumbing down of society. It is mind pollution."

– John McCabe

"How do you expect to have peace within if you are eating slaughtered animals? Simply follow a vegan diet and you will be far better off."

– John McCabe

"If anyone wants to save the planet, all they have to do is just stop eating meat. That's the single most important thing you could do. It's staggering when you think about it. Vegetarianism takes care of so many things in one shot: ecology, famine, cruelty."

– Paul McCartney

"I love to hear a choir. I love the humanity to see the faces of real people devoting themselves to a piece of music. I like the teamwork. It makes me feel optimistic about the human race when I see them cooperating like that."

– Paul McCartney

"We stopped eating meat many years ago. During the course of a Sunday lunch we happened to look out of the kitchen window at our young lambs playing happily in the fields. Glancing down at our plates, we suddenly realised we were eating the leg of an animal who had until recently been playing in a field herself. We looked at each other and said: 'Wait a minute, we love these sheep, they're such gentle creatures. So why are we eating them?' It was the last time we ever did."

– Paul and Linda McCartney

"It is better to have a meaningful life and make a difference than to merely have a long life."

– Bryant H. McGill

"When you choose to view your stress response as helpful, you create the biology of courage. And when you choose to connect with others under stress, you can create resilience."

– Kelly McGonigal

"It may take courage to embrace the possibilities of your own potential, but once you've flown past the summit of your fears, nothing will seem impossible."
– Michael McKee

"Reclaim your mind and get it out of the hands of the cultural engineers who want to turn you into a half-baked moron consuming all this trash that's being manufactured out of the bones of a dying world."
– Terence McKenna

"We have to create culture, don't watch TV, don't read magazines, don't even listen to NPR. Create your own roadshow. The nexus of space and time where you are now is the most immediate sector of your universe, and if you're worrying about Michael Jackson or Bill Clinton or somebody else, then you are disempowered, you're giving it all away to icons, icons which are maintained by an electronic media so that you want to dress like X or have lips like Y. This is shit-brained, this kind of thinking. That is all cultural diversion, and what is real is you and your friends and your associations, your highs, your orgasms, your hopes, your plans, your fears. And we are told 'no', we're unimportant, we're peripheral. 'Get a degree, get a job, get a this, get a that.' And then you're a player, you don't want to even play in that game. You want to reclaim your mind and get it out of the hands of the cultural engineers who want to turn you into a half-baked moron consuming all this trash that's being manufactured out of the bones of a dying world."
– Terence McKenna

"You are an explorer, and you represent our species, and the greatest good you can do is to bring back a new idea, because our world is endangered by the absence of

good ideas. Our world is in crisis because of the absence of consciousness."
– Terence McKenna

"We are caged by our cultural programming. Culture is a mass hallucination, and when you step outside the mass hallucination you see it for what it's worth."
– Terence McKenna

"A point of view can be a dangerous luxury when substituted for insight and understanding."
– Marshall McLuhan

"Anyone who tries to make a distinction between education and entertainment doesn't know the first thing about either."
– Marshall McLuhan

"Most of our assumptions have outlived their uselessness."
– Marshall McLuhan -

"The story begins only when the book closes."
– Marshall McLuhan

"If we are to achieve a richer culture, rich in contrasting values, we must recognize the whole gamut of human potentialities, and so weave a less arbitrary social fabric, one in which each diverse human gift will find a fitting place."
– Margaret Mead

"The future is not some place we are going to, but one we are creating."
– Julia Melchor

"The real measure of your wealth is how much you'd be worth if you lost all your money."
– Bernard Meltzer

"We cannot live only for ourselves. A thousand fibers connect us with our fellow men; and among those fibers, as sympathetic threads, our actions run as causes, and they come back to us as effects."
– Herman Melville

"He who has never failed somewhere, that man can not be great."
– Herman Melville

"People wait for opportunity to come along...yet it is there every morning."
– Dennis the Menace

"Listening is a magnetic and strange thing, a creative force. The friends who listen to us are the ones we move toward. When we are listened to, it creates us, makes us unfold and expand."
– Karl Augustus Menninger

"Love cures people, both the ones who give it and the ones who receive it."
– Karl Augustus Menninger

"Complain and remain. Praise and be raised."
– Joyce Meyer

"If people knew how hard I worked to achieve my mastery, it wouldn't seem so wonderful after all."
– Michelangelo

"I saw the angel in the marble and carved it until I set him free."
– Michelangelo

"Each one of us can make a difference. Together we make change."
– Barbara Mikulski

"They who know how to employ opportunities will often find that they can create them; and what we can achieve depends less on the amount of time we possess than on the use we make of our time."
– John Stuart Mill

"I have learned to seek my happiness by limiting my desires, rather than in attempting to satisfy them."
– John Stuart Mill

"Contempt is the weapon of the weak and a defense against one's own despises and unwanted feelings."
– Alice Miller

"Example moves the world more than doctrine."
– Henry Miller

"True strength lies in submission which permits one to dedicate his life, through devotion, to something beyond himself."
– Henry Miller

"Art is only a means to life, to the life more abundant. It is not in itself the life more abundant. It merely points the way, something which is overlooked not only by the public, but very often by the artist himself. In becoming an end it defeats itself."
– Henry Miller

"Go out into the world and do good until there is too much good in the world."
– Larry H. Miller

"You probably wouldn't worry about what people think of you if you could know how seldom they do."
– Olin Miller

"Willpower is the key to success. Successful people strive no matter what they feel by applying their will to overcome apathy, doubt or fear."
– Dan Millman

"Those who are the hardest to love, are the ones who need it the most."
– Dan Millman

"Awake, arise or be for ever fall'n."
– John Milton

"We embrace pain and burn it as fuel for our journey.
– Kenji Miyazawa

"Don't talk about yourself; it will be done when you leave."
– Wilson Mizner

"The best day of your life is the one on which you decide your life is your own. No apologies or excuses. No one to lean on, rely on, or blame. The gift is yours – it is an amazing journey and you alone are responsible for the quality of it. This is the day your life really begins."
– Bob Moawad

"Every good act is charity. A man's true wealth hereafter is the good that he does in this world to his fellows."
– Mohammed

"Every good act is charity. A man's true wealth hereafter is the good that he does in this world to his fellows."
– Mohammed

"There's no doubt in my mind that going vegetarian has made me feel better not only physically but also because I learned about the suffering of animals who are raised and killed for food. I feel good knowing I'm not contributing to that."
– Sophie Monk

"I believe that everything happens for a reason. People change so that you can learn to let go, things go wrong so that you appreciate them when they're right, you believe lies so you eventually learn to trust no one but yourself, and sometimes good things fall apart so better things can fall together."
– Marilyn Monroe

"Keep smiling, because life is a beautiful thing and there's so much to smile about."
– Marilyn Monroe

"Food preparation is a language, and a meal is a story."
– Richard K Moore

"Unconditional love is our birthright, not judgment or condemnation, and there's nothing we need to do to earn it. This is simply who and what we are."
– Anita Moorjani

"Sometimes a breakdown can be the beginning of a kind of breakthrough, a way of living in advance through a trauma that prepares you for a future of radical transformation."
– Cherrie Moraga

"Obstacles are those frightful things you see when you take your eyes off the goal."
– Hannah More

"There is only one success – to be able to spend your life in your own way."
– Christopher Morley

"The irony of commitment is that it's deeply liberating in work, in play, in love."
– Anne Morriss

"To keep from getting too far ahead of myself, I can apply to life what I've learned from running in the woods: the step in front of you is the most important one."
– Annie Morris

"That's what real love amounts to – letting a person be what he really is. Most people love you for who you pretend to be. To keep their love, you keep pretending – performing. You get to love your pretense. It's true, we're locked in an image, an act."
– Jim Morrison

"The theme you choose may change or simply elude you, but being your own story means you can always choose the tone. It also means you can invent the language to say who you are and what you mean."
– Toni Morrison

"The first thing you have to know about writing is that it is something you must do everyday. There are two reasons for this rule: Getting the work done and connecting with your unconscious mind."

– Walter Mosley

"I think it is necessary to have many experiences for the sake of feeling something; for the sake of being challenged, and for the sake of being expressive, to offer something to someone else, to learn what we are capable of."

– Jason Mraz

"Climb the mountains and get their good tidings. Nature's peace will flow into you as sunshine flows into trees. The winds will blow their own freshness into you, and the storms their energy, while cares will fall off like autumn leaves."

– John Muir

"When we try to pick out anything by itself, we find it hitched to everything else in the Universe."

– John Muir

"When one tugs at a single thing in nature, he finds it attached to the rest of the world."

– John Muir

"Within sorrow is grace. When we come close to those things that break us down, we touch those things that also break us open. And in that breaking open, we uncover our true nature."

– Wayne Muller

"Take wrong turns. Talk to strangers. Open unmarked doors. And if you see a group of people in a field, go find out what they are doing. Do things without always knowing how they'll turn out. You're curious and smart and bored, and all you see is the choice between working hard and slacking off. There are so many adventures that you miss because you're waiting to think of a plan. To find them, look for tiny interesting choices. And remember that you are always making up the future as you go."

– Randall Munroe

"And once the storm is over, you won't remember how you made it through, how you managed to survive. You won't even be sure, whether the storm is really over. But one thing is certain. When you come out of the storm, you won't be the same person who walked in."

– Haruki Murakami

"If you live in the past, you won't have a future."

– Russell Murphy

"Make every minute count, but don't keep score."

– Russell Murphy

"To be persuasive we must be believable; to be believable we must be credible; to be credible we must be truthful."

– Edward R. Murrow

"A nation of sheep will soon have a government of wolves."

– Edward R. Murrow

"The entire physical world is nothing more than our classroom, and the challenge is for us to decide whether to make choices that enhance our spirit or drain our power."

– Caroline Myss

# N

"Just go out there and do what you've got to do."
– Martina Navratilova

"If you have not often felt the joy of doing a kind act, you have neglected much, and most of all yourself."
– A. Neilen

"If you can't afford to do something right, then make darn sure you can afford to do it wrong."
– Charlie Nelson

"Once you replace negative thoughts with positive ones, you'll start having positive results."
– Willie Nelson

"You are the generation about to come into control and must prepare for this responsibility. Do not fill up your leisure with meaningless activity or with causes. Have the courage to stand aside and watch for a little while. It is more important to know where we are going than to get there quickly. Do not mistake activity for achievement."
– Mabel Newcomer

"We are living in a world today where lemonade is made from artificial flavors, and furniture polish is made from real lemons."
– Alfred E. Newman

"Ability hits the mark where presumption overshoots and diffidence falls short."
– John Henry Newman

"I do not know what I may appear to the world, but to myself I seem to have been only like a boy playing on the sea-shore, and diverting myself now and then finding a smoother pebble or a prettier shell than ordinary, whilst the great ocean of truth lay all undiscovered before me."
– Isaac Newton

"The difference between a mountain and a molehill is your perspective."
– Al Neuharth

"Honest towards ourselves and towards anyone else who is our friend; brave towards the enemy; magnanimous towards the defeated; polite always: this is how the four cardinal virtues want us to act."
– Friedrich Nietzsche

"If you gaze for long into the abyss, the abyss also gazes into you."
– Friedrich Wilhelm Nietzsche

"As long as you still experience the stars as something 'above you,' you lack the eye of knowledge."
– Friedrich Nietzsche

"I am not to be a herdsman, I am not to be a grave-digger. Not any more will I discourse unto the people; for the last time have I spoken unto the dead. With the creators, the reapers, and the rejoicers will I associate: the rainbow will I show them, and all the stairs to the Superman."
– Friedrich Nietzsche

"Distrust all in whom the impulse to punish is powerful."
– Friedrich Nietzsche

"He who fights with monsters should look to it that he himself does not become a monster. When you gaze into the abyss, the abyss also gazes into you."
– Friedrich Nietzsche

"Possessions are generally diminished by possession."
– Friedrich Nietzsche

"Sometimes people don't want to hear the truth because they don't want their illusions destroyed."
– Friedrich Nietzsche

"Sometimes people don't want to hear the truth, because they don't want their illusion destroyed."
– Friedrich Nietzsche

"It is not when truth is dirty, but when it is shallow, that the lover of knowledge is reluctant to step into its waters."
– Friedrich Nietzsche

"Am I motivated by what I really want out of life – or am I mass-motivated?"
– Earl Nightingale

"A great attitude does much more than turn on the lights in our worlds: it seems to magically connect us to all sorts of serendipitous opportunities that were somehow absent before the change."
– Earl Nightingale

"Whatever your dominant personal reason, you will find that reading gives knowledge, creative power, satisfaction and relaxation. It cultivates your mind by calling its faculties into exercise.

Books are a source of pleasure - the purest and the most lasting. They enhance your sensation of the interestingness of life. Reading them is not a violent pleasure like the gross enjoyment of an uncultivated mind, but a subtle delight.

Reading dispels prejudices which hem our minds within narrow spaces. One of the things that will surprise you as you read good books from all over the world and from all times of man is that human nature is much the same today as it has been ever since writing began to tell us about it.

Some people act as if it were demeaning to their manhood to wish to be well-read but you can no more be a healthy person mentally without reading substantial books than you can be a vigorous person physically without eating solid food. Books should be chosen, not for their freedom from evil, but for their possession of good. Dr. Johnson said: "Whilst you stand deliberating which book your son shall read first, another boy has read both."

– Earl Nightengale

"I do not like eating meat because I have seen lambs and pigs killed. I saw and felt their pain. They felt the approaching death. I could not bear it. I cried like a child. I ran up a hill and could not breath. I felt that I was choking. I felt the death of the lamb."

– Vaslav Nijinsky

"And the time came when the risk to remain tight in a bud was more painful than the risk it took to blossom."

– Anais Nin

"We are like sculptors, constantly carving out of others the image we long for, need, love or desire, often against reality, against their benefit, and always, in the end, a disappointment, because it does not fit them."

– Anais Nin

"Life shrinks or expands in proportion to one's courage."

– Anais Nin

"Each friend represents a world in us, a world possibly not born until they arrive, and it is only by this meeting that a new world is born."

– Anais Nin

"You must have long term goals to keep you from being frustrated by short term failures."

– Charles C. Noble

"It may seem absurd to believe that a 'primitive' culture in the Himalaya has anything to teach our industrialized society. But our search for a future that works keeps spiraling back to an ancient connection between ourselves and the earth, and interconnectedness that ancient cultures have never abandoned."
– Helena Norberg-Hodge

"I don't eat junk foods and I don't think junk thoughts."
– Mildred "Peace Pilgrim" Norman

"To solve the problems of today, we must focus on tomorrow."
– Erik Nupponen

# O

"Nobody in life gets exactly what they thought they were going to get. But if you work really hard and you're kind, amazing things will happen."
– Conan O'Brien

"When people undermine your dreams, predict your doom, or criticize you, remember they're telling you their story, not yours."
– Cynthia Occelli

"No one else sees your life in the way that you do. No one else feels your life in the way that you do. You are the unique inhabitant of your own reality and of your own life."
– John O'Donohue

"Stories can conquer fear, you know. They can make the heart bigger."
– Ben Okri

"The most authentic thing about us is our capacity to create, to overcome, to endure, to transform, to love, and to be greater than our suffering."
– Ben Okri

"Instructions for living a life: Pay attention. Be astonished. Tell about it."
– Mary Oliver

"Go to a classical music concert where one of the instruments is out of tune and then tell me what it sounded like. Mankind is one big orchestra, grossly out of tune with the environment and each other. The music that arises from it is painful to my ears. How about yours? Once you are in tune, stay in tune. Don't let a hundred or a thousand others who are out of tune tell you that you need to tune up."
– Guru Om

"The way we talk to our children becomes their inner voice."
– Peggy O'Mara

"The only person who can really motivate you is you."
– Shaquille "Shaq" O'Neal

"The foolish man seeks happiness in the distance; the wise grows it under his feet."
– James Openheim

"What I've experienced is that I can't know the future. I can't know if anything that I do will change what happens tomorrow. I can't know with certainty, but what I do know is if I do nothing, nothing will change."
– James Orbinski

"Those who are desperate to find love search in vain for their soulmate. Those who desire happiness search for the best within themselves, then their soulmate finds them."
– Charles J. Orlando

"The heart of human excellence often begins to beat when you discover a pursuit that absorbs you, frees you, challenges you, or gives you a sense of meaning, joy, or passion."
– Terry Orlick

"One of the annoying things about believing in free will and individual responsibility is the difficulty of finding somebody to blame your problems on. And when you do find somebody, it's remarkable how often his picture turns up on your driver's license."
– P.J. O'Rourke

"Trees are the best monuments that a man can erect to his own memory. They speak his praises without flattery, and they are blessings to children yet unborn."
– Lord Orrery

"Political language is designed to make lies sound truthful and murder more respectable."
– George Orwell

"Vegetarianism functioned as a purification. When you eat animals you are more under the law of necessity. You are heavy, you gravitate more towards the earth.

When you are a vegetarian you are light and you are more under the law of grace, under the law of power, and you start gravitating towards the sky."

– Osho

"The greatest fear in the world is of the opinions of others and the moment you are unafraid of the crowd, you are no longer a sheep, you become a lion. A great roar arises in your heart, the roar of freedom."

– Osho

"Love is the food of the soul, but you have been starved. Your soul has not received love at all, so you don't know the taste."

– Osho

"The greatest fear in the world is of the opinions of others and the moment you are unafraid of the crowd, you are no longer a sheep, you become a lion. A great roar arises in your heart, the roar of freedom."

– Osho

"You need to associate with people that inspire you, people that challenge you to rise hither, people that make you better. Don't waste your valuable time with people that are not adding to your growth. Your destiny is too important."

– Joel Osteen

"We are all functioning at a small fraction of our capacity to live life fully in its total meaning of loving, caring, creating, and adventuring. Consequently, the actualizing of our potential can become the most exciting adventure of our lifetime."

– Herbert A. Otto

"Certain scholars called correctors cut out of the gospels teaching of our lord Jesus, which they did not propose to follow. Namely, those against the eating of flesh."

– Gideon Jasper Richard Ousley

"Perhaps the most important thing we can undertake toward the reduction of fear is to make it easier for people to accept themselves, to like themselves."

– Bonaro W. Overstreet

"When you come to the edge of all the light you have, and must take a step into the darkness of the unknown, believe that one of two things will happen. Either there will be something solid for you to stand on, or you will be taught how to fly."

– Patrick Overton

"We all have dreams. But in order to make dreams come into reality, it takes an awful lot of determination, dedication, self-discipline, and effort."

– Jesse Owens

"The battles that count aren't the ones for gold medals. The struggles within yourself – the invisible battles inside all of us – that's where it's at."

– Jesse Owens

# P

"There are pervasive stereotypes about masculinity and femininity that define how we are all supposed to act, dress, and speak, and they serve no one. Anyone who defies these so-called norms becomes worthy of comment and scrutiny, and the LGBT community knows this all too well."
– Ellen Page

"The world is my country, all mankind are my brethren, and to do good is my religion."
– Thomas Paine

"Character is much easier kept than recovered."
– Thomas Paine

"Nothing of me is original. I am the combined effort of everybody I've ever known."
– Chuck Palahniuk

"The need for devotion to something outside ourselves is even more profound than the need for companionship. If we are not to go to pieces or wither away, we must have some purpose in life; for no man can live for himself alone."
– Ross Parmenter

"You must never be fearful about what you are doing when it is right."
– Rosa Parks

"You must never be fearful about what you are doing when it is right."
– Rose Parks

"I have learned over the years that when one's mind is made up, this diminishes fear."
– Rosa Parks

"The way I see it, if you want the rainbow, you gotta put up with the rain."
– Dolly Parton

"I'm not going to limit myself just because people won't accept the fact that I can do something else."
– Dolly Parton

"Chance favors the prepared mind."
– Louis Pasteur

"Can you see your lover for me shining through? Cuz what you see in me, I can see in you. And soon enough, you and me we'll be out of time. And kindness will be all we can leave behind."

– Nimo Patel

"What cannot go forward slips back."

– Gaius V. Paterculus

"Don't do nothing because you can't do everything. Do something. Do anything."

– Colleen Patrick-Goudrau

"Music is moonlight in the gloomy night of life."

– Jean Paul

"We cannot change the cards we are dealt, just how we play the hand."

– Randy Pausch

"The brick walls are there for a reason. The brick walls are not there to keep us out. The brick walls are there to give us a chance to show how badly we want something. Because the brick walls are there to stop the people who don't want it badly enough. They're there to stop the other people."

– Randy Pausch

"We do not remember days, we remember moments."

– Cesare Pavese

"To live a creative life, we must lose our fear of being wrong."

– Joseph Chilton Pearce

"Become a possibilitarian. No matter how dark things seem to be or actually are, raise your sights and see possibilities – always see them, for they're always there."

– Norman Vincent Peale

"Empty pockets never held anyone back. Only empty heads and empty hearts can do that."

– Norman Vincent Peale

"The truth is that our finest moments are most likely to occur when we are feeling deeply uncomfortable, unhappy, or unfulfilled. For it is only in such moments, propelled by our discomfort, that we are likely to step out of our ruts and start searching for different ways and truer answers."

– M. Scott Peck

"I expect to pass through life but once. If therefore, there be any kindness I can show, or any good things I can do to any fellow being, let me do it now, and not defer or neglect it, as I shall not pass this way again."

– William Penn

"The ultimate test of a relationship is to disagree but to hold hands."

– Alexandria Penney

"The United States spends over $87 billion conducting a war in Iraq while the United Nations estimates that for less than half that amount we could provide clean water, adequate diets, sanitation services, and basic education to every person on the planet."

– John Perkins

"The need for devotion to something outside ourselves is even more profound than the need for companionship. If we are not to go to pieces or wither away, we must have some purpose in life; for no man can live for himself alone."
– Ross Permenter

"Excellent firms don't believe in excellence – only in constant improvement and constant change."
– Thomas J. Peters

"Walk with the dreamers, the believers, the courageous, the cheerful, the planners, the doers, the successful people with their heads in the clouds and their feet on the ground. Let their spirit ignite a fire within you to leave this world better than when you found it."
– Wilfred Peterson

"The art of being yourself at your best is the art of unfolding your personality into the person you want to be."
– Wilfred A. Peterson

"Success is focusing the full power of all you are on what you have a burning desire to achieve."
– Wilferd A. Peterson

"Appreciation is yeast, lifting ordinary to extraordinary."
– Mary-Ann Petro

"Now the alternative to despair is courage. And human life can be viewed as a continuous struggle between these two options. Courage is the capacity to affirm one's life in spite of the elements which threaten it. The fact that courage usually predominates over despair in itself tells us something important about life. It

tells you that the forces that affirm life are stronger than those that negate it."
– Paul E. Pfuetze

"Food is the most widely abused anti-anxiety drug in America, and exercise is the most potent yet underutilized antidepressant."
– Bill Phillips

"The less you talk, the more you're listened to."
– Pauline Phillips

"What is defeat? Nothing but education; nothing but the first step to something better."
– Wendell Phillips

"Be kind for everyone you meet is fighting a great battle."
– Philo of Alexandria

"I am always doing that which I cannot do, in order that I may learn how to do it."
– Pablo Picasso

"My mother said to me, 'If you are a soldier, you will become a general. If you are a monk, you will become the Pope.' Instead, I was a painter, and became Picasso."
– Pablo Picasso

"There's always going to be bad stuff out there. But here's the amazing thing – light trumps darkness every time. You stick a candle into the dark, but you can't stick the dark into the light."
– Jodi Picoult

"If you realized how powerful your thoughts are, you would never think a negative thought."
– Peace Pilgrim

"When you find peace within yourself, you become the kind of person who can live at peace with others."
– Peace Pilgrim

"Forge your tongue on the anvil of truth."
– Pindar

"What we do for ourselves dies with us. What we do for others and the world is, and remains, immortal."
– Albert Pine

"I've always felt that animals are the purest spirits in the world. They don't fake or hide their feelings, and they are the most loyal creatures on Earth. And somehow we humans think we're smarter – what a joke."
– Pink

"All matter originates and exists only by virtue of a force which brings the particle of an atom to vibration."
– Max Planck

"Be kind, for everyone you meet is fighting a hard battle."
– Plato

"The gods created certain kinds of beings to replenish our bodies; they are the trees and the plants and the seeds."
– Plato

"Music has the capacity to touch the innermost reaches of the soul and music gives flight to the imagination."
– Plato

"As youth fades and time brings changes, we may change many of our present opinions. O let us refrain from setting ourselves up as judge of the highest matters."
– Plato

"This world is indeed a living being endowed with a soul and intelligence, a single visible living entity containing all other living entities, which by their nature are all related."
– Plato

"One can easily understand a child who is afraid of the dark. The real tragedy of life is when grown men and women are afraid of the light."
– Plato

"Perseverance is more prevailing than violence; and many things which cannot be overcome when they are together, yield themselves up when taken little by little."
– Plutarch

"A mind is a fire to be kindled, not a vessel to be filled."
– Plutarch

"The mind is not a vessel to be filled, but a fire to be kindled."
– Plutarch

"Those who dream by day are cognizant of many things which escape those who dream only by night."
– Edgar Allen Poe

"Deep into that darkness peering, long I stood there, wondering… fearing… doubting."
– Edgar Allan Poe

"I want to be around people that do things. I don't want to be around people anymore that judge or talk about what people do. I want to be around people who dream, and support, and do things."
– Amy Poehler

"To repeat what others have said requires education, to challenge it requires a brain."
– Mary Poole

"To be angry is to revenge the faults of others on ourselves."
– Alexander Pope

"Consult not your fears but your hopes and your dreams. Think not about your frustrations, but about your unfulfilled potential. Concern yourself not with what you tried and failed in, but with what it is still possible for you to do."
– Pope John XXIII

"A man should never be ashamed to own he has been in the wrong, which is but saying, in other words, that he is wiser today than he was yesterday."
– Alexander Pope

"Know then thyself, presume not God to scan / the proper study of mankind is man."
– Alexander Pope

"Values are like fingerprints. Nobody's are the same, but you leave 'em all over everything you do."
— Elvis Presley

"People think you are crazy if you talk about things they don't understand."
— Elvis Presley

"Who walks fastest, but walks astray, is only furthest from his way."
— Matthew Prior

"Let's give the historians something to write about."
— Propertius

"Let us be grateful to people who make us happy; they are the charming gardeners who make our souls blossom."
— Marcel Proust

"Most of the time we are only partially alive. Most of our faculties go on sleeping because they rely on habit which can function without them."
— Marcel Proust

"The righteous man has regard for the life of his beast."
— Proverbs 12:10

"Everything great in the world comes from neurotics. They alone have founded our religions and composed our masterpieces. Never will the world know all it owes them nor all they have suffered to enrich us. We enjoy lovely music, beautiful paintings, a thousand intellectual delicacies, but we have no idea their cost, to those who invented them, in sleepless nights, tears,

spasmodic laughter, rashes, asthmas, epilepsies, and the fear of death, which is worse than all the rest."
– Marcel Proust

"The lower is servant to the lender."
– Proverbs 22:7

"You must unlearn what you have been programmed to believe since birth. That software no longer serves you if you want to live in a world where all things are possible!"
– Jacqueline E. Purcell

"You don't win races by wishing, you win them by running faster than everyone else does."
– Philip Pullman

"Respect yourself most of all."
– Pythagoras

"The animals share with us the privilege of having a soul."
– Pythagoras

Q

"Your present circumstances don't determine where you can go; they merely determine where you start."
– Nido Qubein

# R

"One act of beneficence, one act of real usefulness, is worth all the abstract sentiment in the world."
– Ann Radcliff

"Courage doesn't always roar. Sometimes courage is the little voice at the end of the day that says I'll try again tomorrow."
– Mary Anne Radmacher

"Live with intention. Walk to the edge. Listen hard. Practice wellness. Play with abandon. Laugh. Choose with no regret. Appreciated your friends. Continue to learn. Do what you love. Live as if this is all there is."
– Mary Anne Radmacher

"Lean forward into your life. Catch the best bits and the finest wind. Just tip your feathers in flight a wee bit and see how dramatically that small lean can change your life."
– Mary Anne Radmacher

"Courage doesn't always roar. Sometimes courage is the little voice at the end of the day that says I'll try again tomorrow."
– Mary Anne Radmacher

"Religion is for people who are afraid to go to hell. Spirituality, on the other hand, is for those of us who have been there."
– Bonnie Raitt

"Altruism is innate, but it's not instinctual. Everybody's wired for it, but a switch has to be flipped."
– David Rakoff

"You waste the attention of your eyes, the glittering labor of your hands and knead dough for dozens of loaves of which you'll not taste a morsel; you are free to slave for others – you are free to make the rich richer. The moment you're born they plant around you mills that grind lies, lies to last you a lifetime. You keep thinking in your great freedom a finger on your temple free to have a free conscience. There's neither an iron wooden nor tuile curtain in your life; there's no need to choose Freedom; you are free. But this kind of freedom is a sad affair under the stars."
– Nazim Hikmet Ran

"Basic chemistry leaves us in little doubt that our burning of fossil fuels is changing the acidity of our oceans. And the rate of change we are seeing to the ocean's chemistry is a hundred times faster than has happened for millions of years.

Failure to (cut carbon dioxide emissions) may mean there is no place in the oceans of the future for many species and ecosystems that we know today."

– John Raven

"In the long run, the pessimist may be proved right; but the optimist has a better time on the trip."

– Daniel L. Reardon

"A hero is an ordinary individual who finds the strength to persevere and endure in spite of overwhelming obstacles."

– Christopher Reeve

"So many of our dreams at first seem impossible, then they seem improbable, and then when we summon the will, they soon become inevitable."

– Christopher Reeve

"Happiness is an attitude. We either make ourselves miserable or happy or strong. The amount of work is the same."

– Francesca Reigler

"At the deepest level, the creative process and the healing process arise from a single source. When you are an artist, you are a healer; a wordless trust of the same mystery is the foundation of your work and its integrity."

– Rachel Naomi Remen

"And the city had no need of the sun, neither of the moon, to shine in it: for the glory of God did lighten it."

– Revelation 21:23

"To write something, you have to risk making a fool of yourself."
– Anne Rice

"In this country, Christians can teach toddlers to hate and to persecute, and we, through the automatic tax exemption for churches, foot the bill."
– Anne Rice

"Depend upon yourself. Make your judgment trustworthy by trusting it. You can develop good judgment as you do the muscles of your body – by judicious, daily exercise. To be known as a man of sound judgment will be much in your favor."
– Grantland Rice

"Don't wait for extraordinary circumstances to do good; try to use ordinary situations."
– Charles Richter

"They learn tolerance for others' faults through our tolerance of their own."
– Cathy Ridner

"We're finally going to get the bill for the Industrial Age. If the projections are right, it's going to be a big one: the ecological collapse of the planet."
– Jeremy Rifkin

"There are only two options regarding commitment. You're either in or out. There's no such thing as a life in-between."
– Pat Riley

"May what I do flow from me like a river, no forcing and no holding back, the way it is with children."
– Rainer Maria Rilke

"Perhaps all the dragons in our lives are princesses who are only waiting to see us act, just once, with beauty and courage. Perhaps everything that frightens us is, in its deepest essence, something helpless that wants our love."

– Rainer Maria Rilke

"That is the principal thing: not to remain with the dream, with the intention, with the being in the mood, but always forcibly to convert it into all things."

– Rainer Maria Rilke

"If you live for having it all, what you have is never enough."

– Vicki Robin

"Live life fully while you're here. Experience everything. Take care of yourself and your friends. Have fun, be crazy, be weird. Go out and screw up. You're going to anyway, so you might as well enjoy the process. Take the opportunity to learn from your mistakes: find the cause of your problem and eliminate it. Don't try to be perfect; just be an excellent example of being human."

– Anthony Robbins

"A real decision is measured by the fact that you've taken a new action. If there's no action, you haven't truly decided."

– Anthony Robbins

"The quality of your life is the quality of your relationships."

– Anthony Robbins

"Setting goals is the first step in turning the invisible into the visible."
– Anthony Robbins

"There's no abiding success without commitment."
– Anthony Robbins

"Turn off the TV, don't read the newspapers, listen to your own heart, and listen very tenderly to the hearts of those people who are within your circle of care and affection."
– John Robbins

"Stay committed to your decisions, but stay flexible in your approach."
– Tom Robbins

"Education doesn't need to be reformed – it needs to be transformed. The key is not to standardize education, but to personalize it, to build achievement on discovering the individual talents of each child, to put students in an environment where they want to learn and where they can naturally discover their true passions."
– Ken Robinson

"When your brook dries up and disappointment comes your way, you do not necessarily need to assume that you did something wrong."
- Ryan Robles

"Just because people are poor, or have little, doesn't mean that their dreams aren't big and their soul isn't rich. That's where the classes and the prejudices come from is that there is a difference between you and me and there is a difference between them and us."
– Eva Rodriguez

"One of the greatest and simplest tools for learning more and growing is doing more."
– John Roger

"Choose your intention carefully and then practice holding your consciousness to it, so it becomes the guiding light in your life."
– John Roger

"I doubt that we can ever successfully impose values or attitudes or behaviors on our children certainly not by threat, guilt, or punishment. But I do believe they can be induced through relationships where parents and children are growing together. Such relationships are, I believe, built on trust, example, talk, and caring."
– Fred Rogers

"If you could only sense how important you are to the lives of those you meet; how important you can be to the people you may never even dream of. There is something of yourself that you leave at every meeting with another person."
– Fred Rogers

"Over every mountain there is a path, although it may not be seen from the valley."
– James Rogers

"There is nothing as easy as denouncing. It don't take much to see that something is wrong, but it takes some eyesight to see what will put it right again."
– Will Rogers

"Success is nothing more than a few simple disciplines, practiced every day."
– Jim Rohn

"Either you run the day, or the day runs you."
– Jim Rohn

"If you don't design your own life plan, chances are you'll fall into someone else's plan. And guess what they have planned for you? Not much."
– Jim Rohn

"Success is neither magical nor mysterious. Success is the natural consequence of consistently applying the basic fundamentals."
– Jim Rohn

"The purpose of life is to live it, to taste experience to the utmost, to reach out eagerly and without fear for newer and richer experience."
– Eleanor Roosevelt

"Friendship with oneself is all-important, because without it one cannot be friends with anyone else in the world."
– Eleanor Roosevelt

"No one can make you feel inferior without your consent."
– Eleanor Roosevelt

"The future belongs to those who believe in the beauty of their dreams."
– Eleanor Roosevelt

"The heart has reasons that reason does not understand."
– Jacques Benigne Rossuel

"Talent is merely an interest exercised. In other words, you can be good at anything, as long as you like it enough to practice."
– Bob Ross

"I think the purpose of life is to be useful, responsible, honorable, compassionate. It is, above all, to matter: to count, to stand for something, to have made some difference that you lived at all."
– Leo Rosten

"You can understand and relate to most people better if you look at them – no matter how old or impressive they may be – as if they are children. For most of us never really grow up or mature all that much – we simply grow taller. O, to be sure, we laugh less and play less and wear uncomfortable disguises like adults, but beneath the costume is the child we always are, whose needs are simple, whose daily life is still best described by fairy tales."
– Leo Rosten

"It would be an instructive exercise for the skeptical reader to try to frame a definition of taxation which does not also include theft. Like the robber, the State demands money at the equivalent of gunpoint; if the taxpayer refuses to pay, his assets are seized by force, and if he should resist such deprivation, he will be arrested or shot if he should continue to resist."
– Murray Rothbard

"The person who has lived the most is not the one with the most years, but the one with the richest experiences."
– Jean-Jacques Rousseau

"Being wealthy isn't just a question about having lots of money, it's a question of having what we want. Wealth isn't an absolute, it's relative to desire. Every time we seek something that we can't afford we can be counted as poor no matter how much money we may actually have and every time we are satisfied with what we have we can be counted as rich, however little we may actually possess."

– Jean-Jacques Rousseau

"We do not need magic to transform our world. We carry all of the power we need inside ourselves already."

– J.K. Rowling

"Indifference and neglect often do much more damage than outright dislike."

– J.K. Rowling

"Never underestimate the power of dreams and the influence of the human spirit. We are all the same in this notion. The potential for greatness lives within each of us."

– Wilma Rudolph

"We don't blink an eye at the money that we have been spending on perpetual warfare. We literally don't even, we don't sit here and go, 'Whoa, trillions and trillions of dollars for warfare.' But when we're talking about healthcare, which is our people and their well-being, we're shocked that it should cost us some money."

– Mark Ruffalo

"Don't take anything personally. Even when a situation seems so personal, even if others insult you directly, it has nothing to do with you. Their point-of-

view and opinion come from all the programming they received growing up. When you take things personally, you feel offended and your reaction is to defend your beliefs and create conflict. You make something big out of something so little because you have the need to be right and make everyone else wrong."
 – Don Miguel Ruiz

"Let yourself be silently drawn by the strange pull of what you really love. It will not lead you astray."
 – Jalal ad-Din Rumi

"Set your life on fire. Seek those who fan your flames."
 – Jalal ad-Din Rumi

"Let us join our hands. Listen to every flutter of our heart. Let us become one in silence."
 – Jalal ad-Din Rumi

"There is a candle in your heart, ready to be kindled. There is a void in your soul, ready to be filled.
You feel it, don't you?"
 – Jalal ad-Din Rumi

 "The morning wind spreads its fresh smell. We must get up and take that in, that wind that lets us live. Breathe before it's gone."
 – Jalal ad-Din Rumi

"Lovers don't finally meet somewhere, they're in each other all along."
 – Jalal ad-Din Rumi

"Remember, the entrance door to the sanctuary is inside you."
 – Jalal ad-Din Rumi

"Plunge, plunge into the vast ocean of consciousness, let the drop of water that is you become a hundred mighty seas. But do not think that the drop alone becomes the ocean. The ocean, too, becomes a drop."

– Jalal ad-Din Rumi

"Out beyond all notions of right and wrong there is a field. Will you meet me there? When the soul lies down in that grass, the world is too full to talk about. Ideas, language, even the phrase each other doesn't make any sense."

– Jalal ad-Din Rumi

"The wound is the place where the Light enters you."

– Jalal ad-Din Rumi

"Happiness is not a state to arrive at, but a manner of traveling."

– Margaret Lee Runbeck

"No great intellectual thing was ever done by great effort."

– John Ruskin

"When love and skill work together, expect a masterpiece."

– John Ruskin

"One must care about a world one will not see."
– Bertrand Russell

"A world full of happiness is not beyond human power to create; the obstacles imposed by inanimate nature are not insuperable. The real obstacles lie in the heart of man, and the cure for these is a firm hope, informed and fortified by thought."

   – Bertrand Russell

"In all affairs it's a healthy thing now and then to hang a question mark on the things you have long taken for granted."

   – Bertrand Russell

"The whole problem with the world is that fools and fanatics are always so certain of themselves, and wiser people so full of doubt."

   – Bertrand Russell

"All human activity is prompted by desire."

   – Bertrand Russell

"One of the sanest, surest, and most generous joys of life comes from being happy over the good fortune of others."

   – Archibald Rutledge

"Motivation is what gets you started. Habit is what keeps you going."

   – Jim Ryuh

# S

"One of the saddest lessons of history is this: If we've been bamboozled long enough, we tend to reject any evidence of the bamboozle. We're no longer interested in finding out the truth. The bamboozled has captured us. It's simply too painful to acknowledge, even to ourselves, that we've been taken. Once you give a charlatan power over you, you almost never get it back."
– Carl Sagan

"For small creatures such as we, the vastness is bearable only through love."
– Carl Sagan

"If we can't think for ourselves, if we're unwilling to question authority, then we're just putty in the hands of those in power. But if the citizens are educated and form their own opinions, then those in power work for us. IN every country, we should be teaching our children the scientific method and the reasons for a Bill of Rights. With it comes a certain decency, humility, and community spirit. In the demon-haunted world that we inhabit by virtue of being human, this may be all that stands between us and the enveloping darkness."
– Carl Sagan

"I understand that the most important encounter in life is the encounter with oneself."
– Yves Saint Laurent

"People have many illusions that block them from acting in their own best interest. In dealing with the present problems of life, we must first be able to see the reality of our lives."
– Jonas Salk

"Often it's the deepest pain which empowers you to grow into your highest self."
– Karen Salmansohn

"The world is like a mirror; frown at it, and it frowns at you. Smile and it smiles, too."
– Herbert Samuels

"What would you do if you weren't afraid?"
– Sheryl Sandberg

"Time is the coin of your life. It is the only coin you have, and only you can determine how it will be spent. Be careful lest you let other people spend it for you."
– Carl Sandburg

"If you were all alone in the universe with no one to talk to, no one with which to share the beauty of the stars, to laugh with, to touch, what would be your purpose in life? It is other life, it is love, which gives your life meaning. This is harmony. We must discover the joy of each other, the joy of challenge, the joy of growth."
– Mitsugi Saotome

"Work and live to serve others, leave this world a little better than you found it and garner for yourself as much peace of mind as you can. This is happiness."
– David Sarnoff

"Brain cells create ideas. Stress kills brain cells. Stress is not a good idea."
– Richard Saunders

"The fact is that we human beings speak the same language. And the language that we speak is the language of storytelling."
– Harold Scheub

"Change alone is eternal, perpetual, immortal."
– Arthur Schopenhauer

"We forfeit three-fourths of ourselves in order to be like other people."
– Arthur Schopenhauer

"All truth passes through three stages. First, it is ridiculed. Second, it is violently opposed. Third, it is accepted as being self-evident."
– Arthur Schopenhauer

"If you want to know your true opinion of someone, watch the effect produced in you by the first sight of a letter from him."

– Arthur Schopenhauer

"For the thing-in-itself, the will to live, exists whole and undivided in every being, even in the smallest, as completely as in the sum-total of all things that ever were or are or will be."

– Arthur Schopenhauer

"An ounce of practice is generally worth more than a ton of theory."

– EF Schumacher

"How we think shows through in how we act. Attitudes are mirrors of the mind. They reflect thinking."

– David J. Schwartz

"The way you get meaning into your life is to devote yourself to loving others, devote yourself to your community around you, and devote yourself to creating something that gives you purpose and meaning."

– Morrie Schwartz

"As far as men go, it is not what they are that interests me, but what they can become."

– Morrie Schwartz

"Sometimes our light goes out, but is blown again into instant flame by an encounter with another human being.. Each of us owes deepest thanks to those who have rekindled this light."

– Albert Schweitzer

"Joy, sorrow, tears, lamentation, laughter — to all these music gives voice, but in such a way that we are transported from the world of unrest to a world of peace, and see reality in a new way, as if we were sitting by a mountain lake and contemplating hills and woods and clouds in the tranquil and fathomless water."
– Albert Schweitzer

"Even if it's a little thing, do something for those who have need of a man's help, something for which you get no pay but the privilege of doing it. For, remember, you don't' live in a world all your own. Your brothers are here too."
– Albert Schweitzer

"At times our own light goes out and is rekindles by a spark from another person. Each of us has cause to think with deep gratitude of those who have lighted the flame within us."
– Albert Schweitzer

"Trust and honesty is an investment you put in people."
– Rachel Joy Scott

"As long as you live, keep learning how to live."
– Segoyewatha

"Optimism is invaluable for the meaningful life. With a firm belief in a positive future you can throw yourself into the service of that which is larger than you are."
– Martin Seligman

"Adopting the right attitude can convert a negative stress into a positive one."
– Hans Selye

"Wherever there is a human being, there is an opportunity for kindness."
— Marcus Annaeus Seneca

"If a man does not know what port he is steering for, no wind is favorable to him."
— Marcus Annaeus Seneca

"If God adds another day to our life, let us receive it gladly."
— Marcus Annaeus Seneca

"But for the sake of some little mouthfull of meat, we deprive a soul of the sun and light. And of that proportion of life and time it has been born into the world to enjoy."
— Marcus Annaeus Seneca

"It is not because things are difficult that we do not dare. It is because we do not dare that they are difficult."
— Marcus Annaeus Seneca

"If a man does not know what port he is steering for, no wind is favorable to him."
— Marcus Annaeus Seneca

"There is no religion without love, and people may talk as much as they like about their religion, but if it does not teach them to be good and kind to other animals as well as humans, it is all a sham."
— Anna Sewell

"Put your ear down close to your soul and listen hard."
— Anne Sexton

"Be great in act, as you have been in thought."
– William Shakespeare

"No legacy is so rich as honesty."
– William Shakespeare

"We know what we are, but know not what we may be."
– William Shakespeare

"Nothing is, unless our thinking makes it so."
– William Shakespeare

"The fault, dear Brutus, is not in our stars, but in ourselves."
– William Shakespeare

"Though there is madness, there is method in it."
– William Shakespeare

"Women speak two languages - one of which is verbal."
– William Shakespeare

"To thine own self be true."
– William Shakespeare

"Never forget the importance of living with unbridled exhilaration. Never neglect to see the exquisite beauty in all living things. Today, and this very moment, is a gift. Stay focused on your purpose."
– Robin S. Sharma

"Life is no brief candle to me. It is a sort of splendid torch which I have got a hold of for the moment, and I want to make it burn as brightly as possible before handing it on to future generations."
– George Bernard Shaw

"If history repeats itself, and the unexpected always happens, how incapable must Man be of learning from experience!"
– George Bernard Shaw

"No question is so difficult to answer as that which the answer is obvious."
– George Bernard Shaw

"The people who get on in this world are the people who get up and look for the circumstances they want, and, if they can't find them, make them."
– George Bernard Shaw

"A liar's punishment is not in the least that he is not believed, but that he cannot believe anyone else."
– George Bernard Shaw

"After a visit to the beach, it's hard to believe that we live in a material world."
– Pam Shaw

"Each of us makes his own weather, determines the color of the skies in the emotional universe which he inhabits."
– Bishop Fulton J. Sheen

"If something can stop you, you might as well let it."
– Sidney Sheldon

"Think contentment the greatest wealth."
– George Shelley

"Poets are the hierophants of an unapprehended inspiration; the mirrors of the gigantic shadows which futurity casts upon the present; the words which express what they understand not; the trumpets which sing to

battle, and feel not what they inspire; the influence which is moved not, but moves. Poets are the unacknowledged legislators of the world."
– Mary Shelley

"Sometimes your only available transportation is a leap of faith."
– Margaret Shepherd

"Trouble is a part of your life – if you don't share it, you don't give the person who loves you a chance to love you enough."
– Dinah Shore

"You may be disappointed if you fail, but you are doomed if you don't try."
– Beverly Sills

"Dear America, when you tell gay Americans that they can't serve their country openly, or marry the person that they love, you're telling that to kids, too. So don't be shocked and wonder where all these bullies are coming from that are torturing young kids and driving them to kill themselves because they're different. They learned it from you."
– Sarah Silverman

"Nothing's changed my life more. I feel better about myself as a person, being conscious and responsible for my actions and I lost weight and my skin cleared up and I got bright eyes and I just became stronger and healthier and happier. Can't think of anything better in the world to be but be vegan."
– Alicia Silverstone

"Forgiveness is freeing up and putting to better use the energy once consumed by holding grudges, harboring resentments, and nursing unhealed wounds. It is rediscovering the strengths we always had and relocating our limitless capacity to understand and accept other people and ourselves."
– Sidney and Suzanne Simon

"Life's ups and downs provide windows of opportunity to determine your values and goals. Think of using all obstacles as stepping stones."
– Marsha Sinetar

"When nonvegetarians say that 'human problems come first' I cannot help wondering what exactly it is that they are doing for human beings that compels them to continue to support the wasteful, ruthless exploitation of farm animals."
– Peter Singer

"Blushing is the color of virtue."
– Diogenes of Sinope

"Self-acceptance comes from meeting life's challenges vigorously. Don't numb yourself to your trials and difficulties, nor build mental walls to exclude pain from your life. You will find peace not by trying to escape your problems, but by confronting them courageously. You will find peace not in denial, but in victory."
– Swami Sivananda

"This world is your best teacher. There is a lesson in everything. There is a lesson in each experience. Learn it and become wise. Every failure is a stepping stone to success. Every difficulty or disappointment is a trial of

your faith. Every unpleasant incident or temptation is a test of your inner strength. Therefore nil desperandum. March forward hero!"
– Swami Sivananda

"One of the main reasons wealth makes people unhappy is that it gives them too much control over what they experience. They try to translate their own fantasies into reality instead of tasting what reality itself has to offer."
– Philip Slater

"Recovering is different for every individual. But, for me, my mom pointed out that I could live in the past, that I could hold on to what this man did to me and how he hurt me, and I could feel sorry for myself, or I could choose to not give another minute of my life to this man, and move forward and follow my dreams and do everything I have ever wanted to and so that was the route I chose."
– Elizabeth Smart

"To forgive is to set a prisoner free and discover that the prisoner was you."
– Lewis B. Smedes

"There's something very freeing about losing the anchors that have always defined you. Frightening, sad, but exhilarating in a poignant way, as well. You're free to float to the moon and evaporate or sink to the bottom of the deepest ocean. But you're free to explore. Some people confuse that with drifting, I suppose. I like to think of it as growing."
– Deborah Smith

"For me, winning isn't something that happens suddenly on the field when the whistle blows and the crowds roar. Winning is something that builds physically and mentally every day that you train and every night that you dream."
– Emmitt Smith

"You can't reach for anything new if your hands are still full of yesterday's junk."
– Louise Smith

"We spend money that we do not have, on things we do not need, to impress people who do not care."
– Will Smith

"The separation of talent and skill is one of the greatest misunderstood concepts for people who are trying to excel – for people who have dreams and that want to do things. Talents you have naturally. Skill is only developed by hours and hours and hours of beating on your craft."
– Will Smith

"Throughout life people will make you mad, disrespect you, and treat you bad. Let God deal with the things they do, cause hate in your heart will consume you too."
– Will Smith

"Everybody laughs the same in every language because laughter is a universal connection."
– Yakov Smirnoff

"Employ your time in improving yourself by other men's writings so that you shall come easily by what others have labored hard for."
– Socrates

"Do not pressure what is illusory – property and position: all that is gained at the expense of your nerves decade after decade and can be confiscated in one fell night. Live with a steady superiority over life."
– Alexander Solzhenitsyn

"The quote is always fascinating because it changes out of context, becomes different and sometimes more mysterious. It has a directness and assertiveness it may not have had in the original."
– Susan Sontag

"Defeat should never be a source of discouragement, but rather a fresh stimulus."
– Robert South

"Always desire to learn something useful."
– Sophocles

"If you're never scared or embarrassed or hurt, it means you never take any chances."
– Julia Sorel

"Develop your own compass, and trust it. Take risks, dare to fail, remember the first person through the wall always gets hurt."
– Aaron Sorkin

"You can't live your life for other people. You've got to do what's right for you, even if it hurts some people you love."
– Nicholas Sparks

"Carry out a random act of kindness, with no expectation of reward, safe in the knowledge that one day someone might do the same for you."
– Diana Spencer

"One and the same thing can at the same time be good, bad, and indifferent, e.g., music is good to the melancholy, bad to those who mourn, and neither good nor bad to the deaf."
– Baruch Spinoza

"Blessedness is not the reward of virtue but virtue itself."
– Baruch Spinoza

"Peace is not an absence of war, it is a virtue, a state of mind, a disposition for benevolence, confidence, justice."
– Baruch Spinoza

"Children who grow up getting their nutrition from plant foods rather than meats have a tremendous health advantage. They are less likely to develop weight problems, diabetes, high blood pressure, and some forms of cancer."
– Benjamin Spock, M.D.

"The problem with the way the educational system is set up is that it only recognizes a certain type of intelligence, and it's incredibly restrictive – very, very restrictive. There's so many types of intelligence, and people who would be their best outside of that structure get lost."
– Bruce Springstein

"No one ever did anything worth doing unless he was prepared to go on with it long after it became something of a bore."
– Douglas V. Steere

"Talent can't be taught, but it can be awakened."
– Wallace Stegner

"The first step to getting the things you want out of life is this: Decide what you want."
– Ben Stein

"The truth will set you free. But first, it will piss you off."
– Gloria Steinem

"A pedestal is as much a prison as any small, confined space."
– Gloria Steinem

"The older physicians grow, the more skeptical they become of the virtues of medicine and the more they are disposed to trust the powers of nature."
– Dr. Alexander H. Stevens

"Keep your fears to yourself, but share your courage with others."
– Robert Louis Stevenson

"To be rich in admiration and free from envy, to rejoice greatly in the good of others, to love with such generosity of heart that your love is still a dear possession in absence or unkindness – these are the gifts which money cannot buy."
– Robert Louis Stevenson

"I do my best work when I'm in pain and turmoil."
– Sting

"What we do today, right now, will have an accumulated effect on all our tomorrows."
– Alexandra Stoddard

"Have the courage to say no. Have the courage to face the truth. Do the right thing because it is right. These are the magic keys to living your life with integrity."
– W. Clement Stone

"Truth will always be truth, regardless of lack of understanding, disbelief, or ignorance."
– W. Clement Stone

"A health attitude is contagious, but don't wait to catch it from others. Be a carrier."
– Tom Stoppard

"You need to be aware of what others are doing, applaud their efforts, acknowledge their successes, and encourage them in their pursuits. When we all help one another, everybody wins."
– Jim Stovall

"There are in this world blessed souls, whose sorrows all spring up into joys for others; whose earthly hopes, laid in the grave with many tears, are the seed from which spring healing flowers and balm for the desolate and the distressed."
– Harriet Beecher Stowe

"Men who do things without being told draw the most wages."
– Edwin H. Stuart

"The more conscious you become, the more unconscious you realize you are. You don't stop. There is no stopping place. There is an openness that is part of a new style of thinking."
– Patricia Sun

"Flesh and bone cannot contain the electrical energy that physically operates our body. To me, that is a physical, tangible, real sign of a soul, or that there is something unique in all of us that does not die."
– Patrick Swayze

"The longer I live, the more I realize the impact of attitude on life."
– Charles Swindoll

"Life is ten percent what happens to me and ninety percent how I react to it."
– Charles R. Swindoll

"Practice is the best of all instructors."
– Publius Syrus

"It is not every question that deserves an answer."
– Publilius Syrus

"He is the most free from danger, who, even when safe, is on his guard."
– Publilius Syrus

"Valor grows by daring, fear by holding back."
– Publilius Syrus

"No one reaches a high position without daring."
– Publilius Syrus

"The prompter the refusal, the less the disappointment."
– Publilius Syrus

"Whatever man does he must do first in the mind."
– Albert Szent-Gyorgyi

# T

"It's always the challenge of the future, this feeling of excitement, that drives me."
– Yoshihisa Tabuchi

"The desire for safety stands against every great and noble enterprise."
– Publius Cornelius Tacitus

"The desire for safety stands against every great and noble enterprise."
– Publius Cornelius Tacitus

"When you came you cried and everybody smiled with joy; when you go smile and let the world cry for you."
– Rabindranath Tagore

"Everything comes to us that belongs to us if we create the capacity to receive it."
– Rabindranath Tagore

"If you can't change your fate, change your attitude."
– Amy Tan

"During a very busy life I have often been asked, 'How did you manage to do it all?' The answer is very simple. It is because I did everything promptly."
– Richard Tangye

"We humans are prone to err, and to err systematically, outrageously, and with utter confidence. We are also prone to hold our mistaken notions dear, protecting and nourishing them like our own children. We defend them at great cost. We surround ourselves with safe people, people who will appreciate our cherished views. We avoid those who suggest that our exalted ideas, our little emperors, have no clothes."
– Valerie Tarico

"Our moment in history is indeed a pregnant one. As a civilization and as a species we have come to a moment of truth, which is the future of the human spirit, and the future of the planet, hanging in the balance. If ever boldness, depth, and clarity of vision were called for, from many, it is now."
– Richard Tarnas

"It's not the having, it's the getting."
– Elizabeth Taylor

"Your thoughts, words, and deeds are painting the world around you."
– Jewel Diamond Taylor

"The happiness of a man in this life does not consist in the absence, but in the mastery, of his passions."
– Alfred Tennyson

"There is more hunger for love and appreciation in this world than for bread."
– Mother Teresa

"Work is about a search for daily meaning as well as daily bread, for recognition as well as cash, for astonishment rather than torpor; in short, for a sort of life rather than a Monday through Friday sort of dying."
– Studs Terkel

"My brain is only a receiver. In the universe there is a core from which we obtain knowledge, strength, inspiration. I have not penetrated into the secrets of this core, but I know that it exists."
– Nicola Tesla

"To endure is greater than to dare; to tire out the hostile fortune; to be daunted by no difficulty; to keep heart when all have lost it – who can say this is not greatness?"
– William Makepeace Thackeray

"The universe is always speaking to us, sending us little messages, causing coincidences and serendipities, reminding us to stop, to look around, to believe in something else, something more."
– Nancy Thayer

"Each small task of everyday life is part of the total harmony of the universe."
– St. Theresa of Lisieux

"If those who lead you say to you, 'See, the kingdom is in the sky,' then the birds of the sky will precede you. If they say to you, 'It is in the sea,' then the fish will precede you. Rather, the kingdom is inside of you, and it is outside of you. When you come to know yourselves, then you will become known, and you will realize that it is you who are the sons of the living father. But if you will not know yourselves, you dwell in poverty and it is you who are that poverty."
–Thomas, Gospel of

"Recognize what is in your sight, and that which is hidden from you will become plain to you. For there is nothing hidden which will not become manifest."
–Thomas, Gospel of

"Help people become more motivated by guiding them to the source of their own power."
– Paul G. Thomas

"Music is the effort we make to explain to ourselves how our brains work. We listen to Bach transfixed because this is listening to a human mind."
– Lewis Thomas

"So we shall let the reader answer this question for himself: who is the happier man, he who has braved the storm of life and lived or he who has stayed securely on shore and merely existed?"
– Hunter S. Thompson

"I have no doubt that it is a part of the destiny of the human race, in its gradual improvement, to leave off eating animals."
– Henry David Thoreau

"If men could combine thus earnestly, and patiently, and harmoniously to some really worthy end, what might they not accomplish?"
– Henry David Thoreau

"It is worth the while to live respectably unto ourselves. We can possibly get along with a neighbor, even with a bedfellow, whom we respect very little; but as soon as it comes to this, that we do not respect ourselves, then we do not get along at all."
– Henry David Thoreau

"It is never too late to give up our prejudices."
– Henry David Thoreau

"Go confidently in the direction of your dreams! Live the life you've imagined. As you simplify your life, the laws of the universe will be simpler; solitude will not be solitude, poverty will not be poverty, nor weakness weakness."
– Henry David Thoreau

"There is no remedy for love, but to love more."
– Henry David Thoreau

"We are what we repeatedly do; therefore, excellence is not an act, but a habit."
– Henry David Thoreau

"If a man does not keep pace with his companions, perhaps it is because he hears a different drummer. Let him step to the music which he hears, however measured or far away."

– Henry David Thoreau

"When it comes to die, let us not discover that we have never lived."

– Henry David Thoreau

"Good for the body is the work of the body, good for the soul the work of the soul, and good for either the work of the other."

– Henry David Thoreau

"Let nothing stand between you and the light."

– Henry David Thoreau

"In the long run, men hit only what they aim at. Therefore, they had better aim at something high."

– Henry David Thoreau

"Cultivate a tree which you have found to bear fruit in your soil. Regard not your past failures or successes. All the past is equally a failure and a success; it is a success in as much as it offers you the present opportunity."

– Henry David Thoreau

"I went to the woods because I wished to live deliberately, to front only the essential facts of life, and see if I could not learn what it had to teach, and not, when I came to die, discover that I had not lived."

– Henry David Thoreau

"When our life ceases to be inward and private, conversation degenerates into mere gossip."
– Henry David Thoreau

"I believe that there is a subtle magnetism, which, if we unconsciously yield to it, will direct us aright."
 – Henry David Thoreau

"It's not what you look at that matters, it's what you see."
– Henry David Thoreau

"What you get by achieving your goals is not as important as what you become by achieving your goals."
– Henry David Thoreau

"Let us not look back in anger, nor forward in fear, but around in awareness."
– James Thurber

"To those who say there is no hope I say, 'Liar.'"
– David Tibet

"First of all there will appear to you, swifter than lightning, the luminous splendor of the colorless light of Emptiness, and that will surround you on all sides. Terrified, you will want to flee from the radiance, and you may well lose consciousness. Try to submerge yourself in that light, giving up all belief in a separate self, all attachment to your illusory ego. Recognize that the boundless Light of this true Reality is your own true self."
– The Tibetan Book of the Dead

"The archetypal forms behind all myths belong to the mystery of the creative ground of everything that is."
– Paul Tillich

"Fill each day with life and heart. There is no pleasure in the world comparable to the delight and satisfaction that a good person takes in doing good."
– John Tilloston

"I've never been poor, only broke. Being poor is a frame of mind. Being broke is only a temporary situation."
– Mike Todd

"It is better to err on the side of daring than the side of caution."
– Alvin Toffler

"To love is to recognize yourself in another."
– Eckhart Tolle

"You are not morally superior to the traffic jam!"
– Eckhart Tolle

"Sometimes letting things go is an act of far greater power than defending or hanging on."
– Eckhart Tolle

"A man can live and be healthy without killing animals for food; therefore, if he eats meat, he participates in taking animal life merely for the sake of his appetite. And to act so is immoral."
– Leo Tolstoy

"Never say anything about yourself you do not want to come true."
– Brian Tracy

"The potential of the average person is like a huge ocean unsailed, a new continent unexplored, a world of possibilities waiting to be released and channeled toward some great good."
– Brian Tracy

"We are the people. We have the potential for power. We must not fool ourselves. We must not mislead ourselves. It takes more than good intentions. It takes commitment. It takes recognizing that at some point in our lives we are going to have to decide that we have a way of life that we follow, and we are going to have to live that way of life...That is the only solution there is for us."
– John Trudell

"Worrying is like a rocking chair, it gives you something to do, but it gets you nowhere."
– Glen Turner

"You can never quit. Winners never quit, and quitters never win."
– Ted Turner

"If you are neutral in situations of injustice, you have chosen the side of the oppressor."
– Desmond Tutu

"Do your little bit of good where you are; it's those little bits of good put together that overwhelm the world."
– Desmond Tutu

"There is not enough time to be nasty."
– Desmond Tutu

"Suppose you were an idiot and suppose you were a member of Congress. But I repeat myself."
– Mark Twain

"I have never let my schooling interfere with my education."
– Mark Twain

"For business reasons, I must preserve the outward sign of sanity."
– Mark Twain

"Politicians and diapers must be changed often, and for the same reason."
– Mark Twain

"Anger is an acid that can do more harm to the vessel in which it is stored than to anything on which it is poured."
– Mark Twain

"Get a bicycle. You will not regret it."
– Mark Twain

"It's easier to fool people than to convince them they have been fooled."
– Mark Twain

"If you have nothing to say, say nothing."
– Mark Twain

"You cannot depend on your judgment when your imagination is out of focus."
– Mark Twain

"Sometimes I wonder whether the world is being run by smart people who are putting us on, or by imbeciles who really mean it."
– Mark Twain

"I have never let my schooling interfere with my education."
– Mark Twain

"When I was a boy on the Mississippi River there was a proposition in a township there to discontinue public schools because they were too expensive. An old farmer spoke up and said if they stopped building the schools they would not save anything, because every time a school was closed a jail had to be built."
– Mark Twain

"When you let go of trying to get more of what you don't really need, it frees up oceans of energy to make a difference with what you have. When you make a difference with what you have it expands."
– Lynn Twist

"When you let go of trying to get more of what you don't really need, it frees up oceans of energy to make a difference with what you have."
– Lynne Twist

"Opportunity's favorite disguise is trouble."
– Frank Tyger

"The problem, often not discovered until late in life, is that when you look for things in life like love, meaning, motivation, it implies they are sitting behind a tree or under a rock. The most successful people in life recognize, that in life they create their own love, they manufacture their own meaning, they generate their own motivation. For me, I am driven by two main philosophies, know more today about the world than I knew yesterday. And lessen the suffering of others. You'd be surprised how far that gets you."

– Neil deGrasse Tyson

"To the mind that is still, the whole universe surrenders."

Lao Tzu

"New beginnings are often disguised as painful endings."

– Lao Tzu

"A man with outward courage dares to die; a man with inner courage dares to live."

– Lao Tzu

"How can you follow the course of your life if you do not let it flow?"

– Lao Tzu

"Silence is a source of great strength.

– Lao Tzu

"At the center of your being you have the answer; you know who you are and you know what you want."

– Lao Tzu

"When you look for it, there is nothing to see. When you listen for it, there is nothing to hear. When you use it, it is inexhaustible."

– Lao Tzu

"New beginnings are often disguised as painful endings."

– Lao Tzu

"Care about what other people think, and you will always be their prisoner."
– Lao Tzu

# U

"We may think we are nurturing a garden, but of course it's our garden that is really nurturing us."
– Jenny Uglow

"Life is uncertain. Eat desert first."
– Ernestine Ulmer

"I stopped eating beef at 13 and stopped eating all meat a few years ago. I would feel guilty knowing that what was on my plate was walking around yesterday. Either I could live with that or stop eating meat. I choose the latter, and I'm happier for it."
– Carrie Underwood

# V

"Use what talents you possess; the woods would be very silent if no birds sang there except those that sang best."
– Henry Van Dyke

"The painter of the future will be a colorist such as has never been seen."
– Vincent Van Gogh

"Music kept me off the streets and out of trouble and gave me something that was mine that no one could take away from me. Music education and families are dealing with the economic times, and I wanted to help them. If I

can help a kid discover a liking, or even a passion for music in their life, then that's a wonderful thing."
– Eddie Van Halen

"I don't believe you have to be better than everybody else. I believe you have to be better than you ever thought you could be."
– Ken Venturi

"Water from the ocean contained in a pot can neither be called an ocean nor a non-ocean, but only a part of the ocean."
– Acharya Vigyand

"To love and be loved is to feel the sun from both sides."
– David Viscott

"Your ultimate goal in life is to become your best self. Your immediate goal is to get on the path that will lead you there."
– David Viscott

"Here's Death, twitching in my ear: 'Live,' says he, 'for I am coming.'"
– Virgil

"Fortune sides with him who dares."
– Virgil

"They are able because they think they are able."
– Virgil

"All the powers in the universe are already ours. It is we who have put our hands before our eyes and cry that it is dark."
– Swami Vivekananda

"Arise, awake, and stop not until the goal is achieved."

– Swami Vivekananda

"Take up one idea. Make that one idea your life. Think of it, dream of it, live on that idea. Let that brain, muscles, nerves, every part of your body be full of that idea and just leave every other idea alone. This is the way to success."

– Swami Vivekananda

"I know of no great men except those who have rendered great service to the human race."

– Voltaire

"It is hard to free fools from the chains they revere."

– Voltaire

"What is tolerance? It is the consequence of humanity. We are all formed of frailty and error; les us pardon reciprocally each other's folly – that is the first law of nature."

– Voltaire

"The comfort of the rich depends upon an abundant supply of the poor."

– Voltaire

"Be soft. Do not let the world make you hard. Do not let the pain make you hate. Do not let the bitterness steal your sweetness. Take price that even though the rest of the world may disagree, you still believe it to be a beautiful place."

– Kurt Vonnegut

"To practice any art, no matter how well or badly, is a way to make your soul grow. So do it."
– Kurt Vonnegut

"Another flaw in the human character is that everybody wants to build and nobody wants to do maintenance."
– Kurt Vonnegut, Jr.

"The quality of the box matters little. Success depends upon the man who sits in it."
– Baron Manfred von Richthofen

"As noble Art has survived noble nature, so too she marches ahead of it, fashioning and awakening by her inspiration. Before Truth sends her triumphant light into the depths of the heart, imagination catches its rays, and the peaks of humanity will be glowing when humid night still lingers in the valleys."
– Johann Friedrich Von Schiller

"Dare to be wrong and to dream."
– Johann Friedrich Von Schiller

"The art of writing is the art of applying the seat of the pants to the seat of the chair."
– Mary Heaton Vorse

"It's a lie to think you're not good enough. It's a lie to think you're not worth anything."
– Nick Vuyicic

# W

"You've got to have a dream, if you want to have a dream come true."
– Dennis Waitley

"Relentless, repetitive self talk is what changes our self-image."
– Denis Waitley

"The greatest gifts you can give your children are the roots of responsibility and the wings of independence."
– Denis Waitley

"One characteristic of winners is they always look upon themselves as a do-it-yourself project."
– Denis Waitley

"Failure should be our teacher, not our undertaker. Failure is delay, not defeat. It is a temporary detour, not a dead end. Failure is something we can avoid only by saying nothing, doing nothing, and being nothing."

– Denis Waitley

"As long as we are persistent in our pursuit of our deepest destiny, we will continue to grow. We cannot choose the day or time when we will fully bloom. It happens in its own time."

– Denis Waitley

"Learn from the past, set vivid, detailed goals for the future, and live in the only moment of time over which you have any control: now."

– Denis Waitley

"You must look within for value, but must look beyond for perspective."

– Denis Waitley

"Success is almost totally dependent upon drive and persistence. The extra energy required to make another effort or try another approach is the secret of winning."

– Dennis Waitley

"No person is your friend who demands your silence or denies your right to grow."

– Alice Walker

"Surfing soothes me, it's always been a kind of Zen experience for me. The ocean is so magnificent, peaceful, and awesome. The rest of the world disappears for me when I'm on a wave."

– Paul Walker

"Seven days without laughter makes one weak."
– Mort Walker

"Listen earnestly to anything your children want to tell you, no matter what. If you don't listen eagerly to the little stuff when they are little, they won't tell you the big stuff when they are big, because to them all of it has always been the big stuff."
– Catherine M. Wallace

"Don't let the fear of falling keep you from knowing the joy of flight."
– Lane Wallace

"Every man dies, but not every man truly lives."
– William Wallace

"Life begins at the end of your comfort zone."
– Neale Donald Walsch

"Yesterday has nothing to do with who you are, only who you thought you were."
– Neale Donald Walsch

"Teach not with your words, but with your actions; not with discussion but with demonstration. For it is what you do that your children will emulate, and how you are that they will become."
– Neale Donald Walsch

"The adventure of life is to learn. The goal of life is to grow. The nature of life is to change. The challenge of life is to overcome. The essence of life is to care. The secret of life is to give. The joy of life is to love."
– William Arthur Ward

"It is wise to direct your anger towards problems –
not people; to focus your energies on answers – not
excuses."
– William Arthur Ward

"All glory comes from daring to begin."
– Eugene F. Ware

"They always say that time changes things, but you
actually have to change them yourself."
– Andy Warhol

"Isn't life a series of images that change as they
repeat themselves?"
– Andy Warhol

"Your outlook affects your outcome."
– John Paul Warren

"The world cares very little about what a man or
woman knows; it is what a man or woman is able to do
that counts."
– Booker T. Washington

"Associate yourself with people of good quality, for
it is better to be alone than to be in bad company."
– Booker T. Washington

"I have learned from experience that the greater part
of our happiness or misery depends on our dispositions
and not on our circumstances."
– Martha Washington

"Don't feel stupid if you don't like what everyone
else pretends to love."
– Emma Watson

"Strong people don't put others down. They lift them up."
— Michael P. Watson

"Forty percent of the fish caught from the oceans is fed to livestock – pigs and chickens are becoming major aquatic predators. The livestock industry is one of the greatest contributors to greenhouse gas emissions ever. The eating of meat is an ecological disaster."
— Paul Watson

"We have a population of seven billion people on the planet right now, and the oceans are dying. The oceans have been so severely diminished that there's a good chance we could kill them. And if the oceans die, we die."
— Paul Watson

"Seafood is simply a socially acceptable form of bush meat. We condemn Africans for hunting monkeys and mammalian and bird species from the jungle, yet the developed world thinks nothing of hauling in magnificent wild creatures like swordfish, tuna, halibut, shark and salmon for our meals. The fact is that the global slaughter of marine wildlife is simply the largest massacre of wildlife on the planet."
— Paul Watson

"I'll tell you what hermits realize. If you go off into a far, far forest and get very quiet, you'll come to understand that you're connected with everything."
— Alan Watts

"Normally, we do not so much look at things as overlook them."
— Alan Watts

"All boundaries are held in common. When you understand this, you see that the sense of being 'me' is exactly the same sensation as being one with the whole cosmos. You do not need to go through some other weird, different, or odd kind of experience to feel in total connection with everything."

– Alan Watts

"You may believe yourself out of harmony with life and its eternal now; but you cannot be, for you are life and exist now – otherwise you would not be here. Hence the infinite Tao is something which you can neither escape by flight, nor catch by pursuit; there is no coming toward it or going away from it; it is, and you are it. So become what you are."

– Alan Watts

"Character is doing the right thing when nobody's looking. There are too many people who think that the only thing that's right is to get by, and the only thing that's wrong is to get caught."

– J.C. Watts

"Don't avoid turbulence. The lift is in the turbulence."

– Chris Waugh

"The trick with opportunities is to identify them quickly, be prepared to take advantage of them, and be confident enough to alter your course to do so. Be Aware, Prepare, Dare."

– Chris Waugh

"Notice what you like to do for fun; you'll get insight that will help drive your career choices."

– Chris Waugh

"Reconsider all your limitations as if they were self-imposed. Many of them are!"
– Chris Waugh

"Your launch begins with a single step. Are you ready?"
– Chris Waugh

"Nobody ever goes to bed at night feeling over-appreciated."
– Chris Waugh

"There will come a time when civilized people will look back in horror on our generation and say, 'Meat eaters!' in disgust, and regard us in the same way we regard cannibals."
– Dennis Weaver

"The intelligent man who is proud of his intelligence is like a condemned man who is proud of his large cell."
– Simone Weil

"Even in my worst moments I would not destroy a Greek statue or a fresco by Giotto. Why anything else then? Why, for example, a moment in the life of a human being who could have been happy for that moment."
– Simone Weil

"When a contradiction is impossible to resolve except by a lie, then we know that it is really a door."
– Simone Weil

"Each day we wake up and make myriad choices that affect others. We clothe ourselves with shirts, pants, and shoes that may have been sewn together by women working in factories fourteen-plus hours a day for a

nonliving wage; we buy products manufactured in ways that destroy forests, pollute waterways, and poison the air; we wash our hair with shampoos that may have been squeezed into the eyes of conscious rabbits or force-fed to them in quantities that kill; and on and on. As Derrick Jensen has written in his book 'The Culture of Make Believe,' 'It's possible to destroy a culture without being aware of its existence. It is possible to commit genocide or ecocide from the comfort of one's living room."
– Zoe Weil

"There is no problem so complex that it cannot simply be blamed on the pilot."
– Dr. Earl Weiner

"Every time I see an adult on a bicycle, I no longer despair for the future of the human race."
– H. G. Wells

"If you're coasting, you're either losing momentum or else you're headed downhill."
– Joan Welsh

"Long before I wrote stories, I listened for stories. Listening for them is something more acute than listening to them. I supposed it's an early form of participation in what goes on. Listening children know stories are there. When their elders sit and begin, children are just waiting and hoping for one to come out, like a mouse from its hole."
– Eudora Welty

"Light yourself on fire with passion and people will come from miles to watch you burn."
– John Wesley

"Do all the good you can, by all the means you can, in all the ways you can, in all the places you can, at all the times you can, to all the people you can, as long as ever you can."
– John Wesley

"There are no good girls gone wrong - just bad girls found out"
– Mae West

"Intelligence is composed mostly of imagination, insight, things that have nothing to do with reason."
– Vivienne Westwood

"Equality is not a concept. It's not something we should be striving for. It's a necessity. Equality is like gravity. We need it to stand on this earth as men and women, and the misogyny that is in every culture is not a true part of the human condition. It is life out of balance, and that imbalance is sucking something out of the soul of every man and woman who's confronted with it. We need equality."
– Joss Whedon

"Do not forward. Do not stop, do not linger in your journey, but strive for the mark set before you."
– George Whitefield

"The art of progress is to preserve order amid change, and to preserve change amid order."
– Alfred North Whitehead

"Infuse your life with action. Don't wait for it to happen. Make it happen. Make your own future. Make your own hope. Make your own love. And whatever your beliefs, honor your creator, not by passively waiting for grace to come down from upon high, but by doing

what you can to make grace happen yourself, right now, right down here on Earth."
– Bradley Whitford

"A morning-glory at my window satisfies me more than the metaphysics of books."
– Walt Whitman

"Let your soul stand cool and composed before a million universes."
– Walt Whitman

"Nothing endures but personal qualities."
– Walt Whitman

"Re-examine all that you have been told. Dismiss that which insults your soul."
– Walt Whitman

"The doors we open and close each day decide the lives we live."
– Flora Whittemore

"Of all sad words of mouth or pen, the saddest are these: it might have been."
– John Greenleaf Whittier

"You may choose to look the other way but you can never say again that you did not know."
– William Wilberforce

"A pat on the back is only a few vertebrae removed from a kick in the pants, but is miles ahead in results."
– Ella Wheeler Wilcox

"One ship drives east and the other drives west by the self same winds that blow. It's the set of the sails and not the gales that determines the way they go."
– Ella Wheeler Wilcox

"Some cause happiness wherever they go, others whenever they go."
– Oscar Wilde

"Children begin by loving their parents; as they grow older they judge them; sometimes they forgive them."
– Oscar Wilde

"Ordinary riches can be stolen, real riches cannot. In your soul are infinitely precious things that cannot be taken from you."
– Oscar Wilde

"To love oneself is the beginning of a lifelong romance."
– Oscar Wilde

"I like to do all the talking myself. It saves time, and prevents arguments."
– Oscar Wilde

"Our ambition should be to rule ourselves, the true kingdom for each one of us; and true progress is to know more, and be more, and to do more."
– Oscar Wilde

"The only thing to do with good advice is pass it on."
– Oscar Wilde

"Keep love in your heart. A life without it is like a sunless garden when the flowers are dead."
– Oscar Wilde

"One does not see anything until one sees its beauty."
– Oscar Wilde

"Every good an excellent thing in the world stands moment by moment on the razor-edge of danger and must be fought for."
– Thornton Wilder

"The best thing about animals is they don't talk much."
– Thornton Wilder

"One we experience the love of an animal a new world opens. We see the world as it could be and should be."
– Anthony Douglas Williams

"Times change. The farmer's daughter now tells jokes about the traveling salesman."
– Carey Williams

"Make no excuses. You don't' have time, because if you use your energy that way, you won't have any energy to deal with what you need to deal with, which is overcoming obstacles and obtaining goals."
– Frances Williams

"You're only given one little spark of madness. You mustn't lose it."
– Robin Williams

"I choose to believe I can and will change the world with my words and thoughts."
– Rod Williams

"I have always depended on the kindness of strangers."
– Tennessee Williams

"Everything we do is infused with the energy with which we do it. If we're frantic, life will be frantic. If we're peaceful, life will be peaceful. And so our goal in any situation becomes inner peace."
– Marianne Williamson

"Teach only love for that is what you are."
– Marianne Williamson

"You must learn a new way to think before you can master a new way to be."
– Marianne Williamson

"Our deepest fear is not that we are inadequate. Our deepest fear is that we are powerful beyond measure. It is our light, not our darkness that most frightens us. We ask ourselves, 'Who am I to be brilliant, gorgeous, talented, fabulous?' Actually, who are you not to be? You are a child of God. Your playing small does not serve the world. There is nothing enlightened about shrinking so that other people won't feel insecure around you. We are all meant to shine, as children do. We were born to make manifest the glory of God that is within us. It's not just in some of us; it's in everyone. And as we let our own light shine, we unconsciously give other people permission to do the same. As we are liberated from our own fear, our presence automatically liberates others."
– Marianne Williamson

"Every thought you have makes up some segment of the world you see. It is with your thoughts, then, that we must work, if your perception of the world is to be changed."
– Marianne Williamson

"In every community, there is work to be done. IN every nation, there are wounds to heal. In every heart, there is power to do it."
– Marianne Williamson

"The world is holy. We are holy. All life is holy. Daily prayers are delivered on the lips of breaking waves, the whisperings of grasses, the shimmering of leaves."
– Terry Tempest Williams

"Education is the mother of leadership."
– Wendell L. Willkie

"There's a lot happening in many of us. I think you have to celebrate every part. It's what you are. You have to try to find all of those secret names."
– Cassandra Wilson

"We need to realize that up until this point we have saved our own species with technology, new developments in agriculture, opening new land – and therefore of course destroying large numbers of other species. We've always found a way around our exponential population growth through technology. When it comes to energy extraction, we've had to develop very high technology and complex systems, and they're getting more complex all the time. We've reached a point where what we have wrought is so complicated and ill planned that we can't handle a lot of it. That takes us to a point where we have to recognize that we're not

going to have any kind of livable planet for ourselves unless we make our environment sustainable – and that includes the living environment. We have to slam on the brakes before we wreck the planet. Which we're about to do."
– E.O. Wilson

"Success in almost any field depends more on energy and drive than it does on intelligence."
– Sloan Wilson

"There are old pilots and there are bold pilots, but there are no old bold pilots."
– W. W. Windstaff

"Even though the canvas of your life is painted with daily experiences, behaviors, reactions, and emotions, you're the one controlling the brush."
– Oprah Winfrey

"One hundred years from now, it will not matter what my bank account was, the sort of house I lived in, or the kind of car I drove, but the world may be different because I was important in the life of a child."
– Forest E. Witcraft

"Don't get involved in partial problems, but always take flight to where there is a free view over the whole single great problem, even if this view is still not a clear one."
– Ludwig Wittgenstein

"Logic is not a body of doctrine, but a mirror-image of the world. Logic is transcendental."
– Ludwig Wittgenstein.

"Uttering a word is like striking a note on the keyboard of the imagination."

– Ludwig Wittgenstein

"The most important things don't fit into words, that's why there's music."

– Rachel Wolchin

"If you are too much about what other people think, you will always be their prisoner."

– Wolf Spirit

"Your life is your message to the world. Make sure it's inspiring."

– Wolf Spirit

"My art has led me into deeper relationship with the Earth. When I am outside painting the landscape I often feel part of it — not just a spectator, but a participant. Perception is participation. The more we perceive, the more we participate. The more we participate, the more we are connected. With connection comes caring."

– Adam Wolpert

"We all have ability. The difference is how we us it."

– Stevie Wonder

"Don't mistake activity for achievement."

– John Wooden

"Things turn out best for the people who make the best of the way things turn out."

– John R. Wooden

"If you do not tell the truth about yourself you cannot tell it about other people."

– Virginia Woolf

"By hook or by crook, I hope that you will possess yourselves of money enough to travel and to idle, to contemplate the future or the past of the world, to dream over books and loiter at street corners and let the line of thought dip deep into the stream"
– Virginia Woolf

"An idea is salvation by imagination"
– Frank Lloyd Wright

"You have to go wholeheartedly into anything in order to achieve anything worth having."
– Frank Lloyd Wright

"Learning the secret of flight from a bird was a good deal like learning the secret of magic from a magician. After you know what to look for you see things that you did not notice when you did not know exactly what to look for."
– Orville Wright

"In flying I have learned that carelessness and overconfidence are usually far more dangerous than deliberately accepted risks."
– Wilbur Wright

"What is chiefly needed is skill rather than machinery."
– Wilbur Wright

# X

"Don't be in such a hurry to condemn a person because he doesn't do what you do, or think as you think. There was a time when you didn't know what you know today."
— Malcolm X

# Y

"Someday all you'll have to light the way will be a single ray of hope, and that will be enough."
– Kobi Yamada

"I think every person has the ability to effect change. Every one of us affects the world constantly through our actions. Through our every thought, our every word, the way that we interact with other people we're constantly affecting the world."
– Adam Yauch, Beastie Boys

"I was always afraid of dying. Always. It was my fear that made me learn everything I could about my airplane and my emergency equipment, and kept me flying

respectful of my machine and always alert in the cockpit."
– Chuck Yeager

"If you want to grow old as a pilot, you've got to know when to push it, and when to back off."
– Chuck Yeager

"All hatred driven hence, the soul recovers radical innocence and learns at last that it is self-delighting, self-appeasing, self-afrighting, and that its own sweet will is Heaven's will."
– William Butler Yeats

"The world is full of magic things, patiently waiting for our senses to grow sharper."
– William Butler Yeates

"The truths – those surprising, amazing, unforeseen truths – which our descendants will discover, are even now all around us, staring us in the eyes, and yet we do not see them."
– Paramhansa Yogananda

"Be afraid of nothing. Giving love to all, feeling the love of God, seeing His presence in everyone, and having but one desire - for His constant presence in the temple of your consciousness - that is the way to live in this world."
– Paramahansa Yogananda

"The world does not owe men a living, but business, if it is to fulfill its ideal, owes men an opportunity to earn a living."
– Owen D. Young

"If we all understand that animals can use their eyes to see, ears so hear, noses to smell, mouths to eat, legs to walk, feathers to fly, fins to swim, genitalia to procreate, bowels to defecate – I'm always perplexed that most people don't believe that they can also use their brains to think, feel, be rational, be aware, be self-aware. Am I supposed to believe that every body part of an animal functions just like it's supposed to except the brain?"

– Gary Yourofsky

"Each of us has much more hidden inside us than we have had a chance to explore. Unless we create an environment that enables us to discover the limits of our potential, we will never know what we have inside of us."

– Muhammad Yunus

# Z

"The best day of your life is the one in which you decide your life is your own. No apologies or excuses. No one to lean on, rely on, or blame. The gift of life is yours; it is an amazing journey; and you alone are responsible for the quality of it."
– Dan Zadra

"Worry is a misuse of imagination."
– Dan Zadra

"Though I might travel afar, I will meet only what I carry with me, for every man/woman is a mirror. We see only ourselves reflected in those around us. Their attitudes and actions are only a reflection of our own. The whole world and its condition has its counter parts

within us all. Turn the gaze inward. Correct yourself and your world will change."
— Kirsten Zambucka

"Do not follow the ideas of others, but learn to listen to the voice within yourself. Your body and mind will become clear and you will realize the unity of all things."
— Dogen Zenji

"People often say that motivation doesn't last. Well, neither does bathing – that's why we recommend it daily."
— Zig Ziglar

"What you get by achieving your goals is not as important as what you become by achieving your goals."
— Zig Ziglar

"Historically, the most terrible things – war, genocide, and slavery – have resulted not from disobedience, but from obedience."
— Howard Zinn

"If you ask me what I came into this life to do, I will tell you: I came to live out loud."
— Emile Zola

# ABOUT THE AUTHOR

John McCabe has written a variety of books relating to health, food, thought, and environmental issues.

McCabe's first book was *Surgery Electives: What to Know Before the Doctor Operates*. It was an exposé of the financial ties of the medical school, hospital, pharmaceutical, and health insurance industries whose unethical business practices result in the deaths of tens of thousands of people in the U.S. every year. The book was endorsed by some congresspersons and by all of the patients' rights groups in North America.

McCabe also wrote a similar book specific for those considering cosmetic surgery. *Plastic Surgery Hopscotch* was published in 1995 and detailed many of the risks involved with the various surgeries.

Realizing that medical care in Western culture is largely the end result of horrible dietary choices, McCabe turned to writing about how a plant-based diet can prevent and reverse a wide variety of diseases while also protecting the environment.

Becoming an advocate for plant-based nutrition free of disease-inducing animal protein, synthetic chemicals, heat-generated toxins, and rancid and fried oils, McCabe wrote books including *Sunfood Diet Infusion*, *Sunfood Traveler*, *Vegan Myth Vegan Truth*, *Hollywood Crew Health Revival Plan*, and *Raw Vegan Easy Healthy Recipes*. He also helped other authors write their books on similar topics.

As a way to expose the dire situation of the damaged environment, including from ocean acidification, mountaintop removal, fracking, tar sands mining, clearcutting, nuclear energy, animal agriculture, monocropping, and the spread of industrial pollutants, and to help educate people on the need for a more sustainable society, including the need to shut down the animal farming cartels and stop the GMO companies, McCabe wrote a little book titled *Extinction: The Death of Waterlife on Planet Earth*. In it, McCabe continues his advocacy for a plant-based diet free.

In tune with healthy living, McCabe wrote a book titled *Igniting Your Life*. The book combines philosophical and motivational quotations from throughout history with commentary relating to leading a healthy, goal-oriented, happy life.

McCabe is the author of *Marijuana & Hemp: History, Uses, Laws, and Controversy*, which details the uses of the world's most useful industrial plant, which can be used for everything from construction materials, to fabric, food, and fuel. The book explains how corrupt politicians have worked with corporate leaders to outlaw industrial hemp farming in the U.S. and many other countries.

# Have you found this book helpful?

Let others know about it.
Post about it on Facebook.
Tweet about it on Twitter.
Snap a photo of the cover and text or email it to a friend.
Write a customer review on the book's Amazon.com
page.
Gift a copy to a friend, relative, neighbor, or associate.
Give a copy to a graduate.
Drop a copy at a homeless shelter.
Leave a copy on someone's doorstep.

Uplift.
Encourage.
Compliment.
Bring good tidings.
Build confidence.

Make a game plan, and play it daily.

www.ingramcontent.com/pod-product-compliance
Lightning Source LLC
Chambersburg PA
CBHW060008050426
42448CB00012B/2667